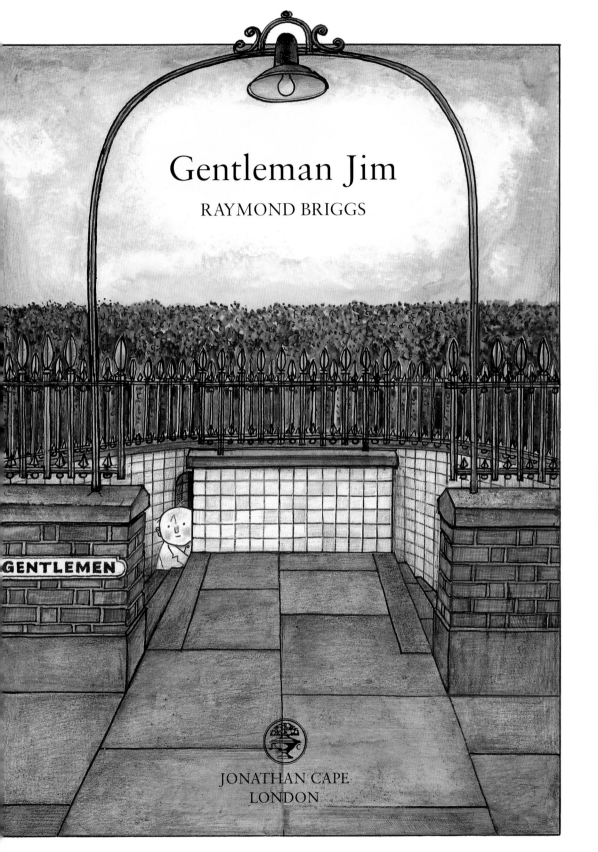

Gentleman Jim

RAYMOND BRIGGS

GENTLEMEN

JONATHAN CAPE
LONDON

Other books by Raymond Briggs

THE STRANGE HOUSE   MIDNIGHT ADVENTURE   SLEDGES TO THE RESCUE
*
RING-A-RING O'ROSES   THE WHITE LAND   FEE FI FO FUM
*
THE MOTHER GOOSE TREASURY   THE FAIRY TALE TREASURY
*
THE ELEPHANT AND THE BAD BABY text by Elfrida Vipont   THE TALE OF THE THREE LANDLUBBERS
JACK AND THE BEANSTALK   FATHER CHRISTMAS   FATHER CHRISTMAS GOES ON HOLIDAY
FUNGUS THE BOGEYMAN   THE SNOWMAN
*
WHEN THE WIND BLOWS   THE TIN-POT FOREIGN GENERAL AND THE OLD IRON WOMAN
UNLUCKY WALLY   ETHEL & ERNEST   UG: THE BOY GENIUS OF THE STONE AGE

Published by Jonathan Cape 2008
Random House,
20 Vauxhall Bridge Road,
London SW1V 2SA

www.rbooks.co.uk

4 6 8 10 9 7 5 3

First published in Great Britain in 1980 by Hamish Hamilton, London

Addresses for companies within The Random House Group Limited can be found at:
www.randomhouse.co.uk/offices.htm

The Random House Group Limited Reg. No. 954009

A CIP catalogue record for this book is available from the British Library

ISBN 9780224085243

Printed and bound in China by C & C Offset Printing Co., Ltd

Gentleman Jim

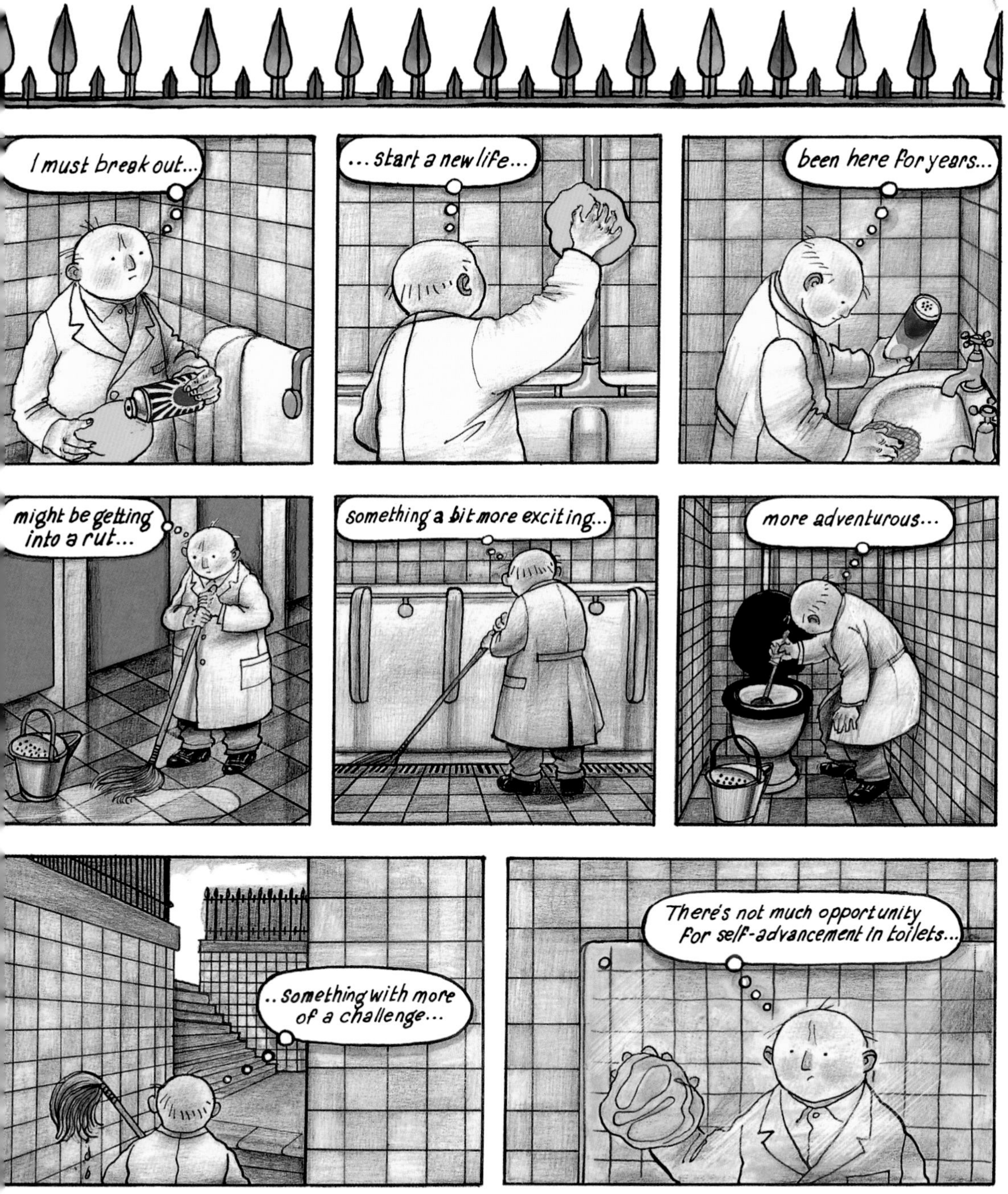
I must break out...
... start a new life...
been here for years...
might be getting into a rut...
something a bit more exciting...
more adventurous...
.. something with more of a challenge...
There's not much opportunity for self-advancement in toilets...

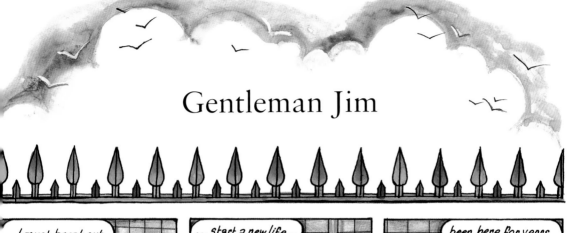

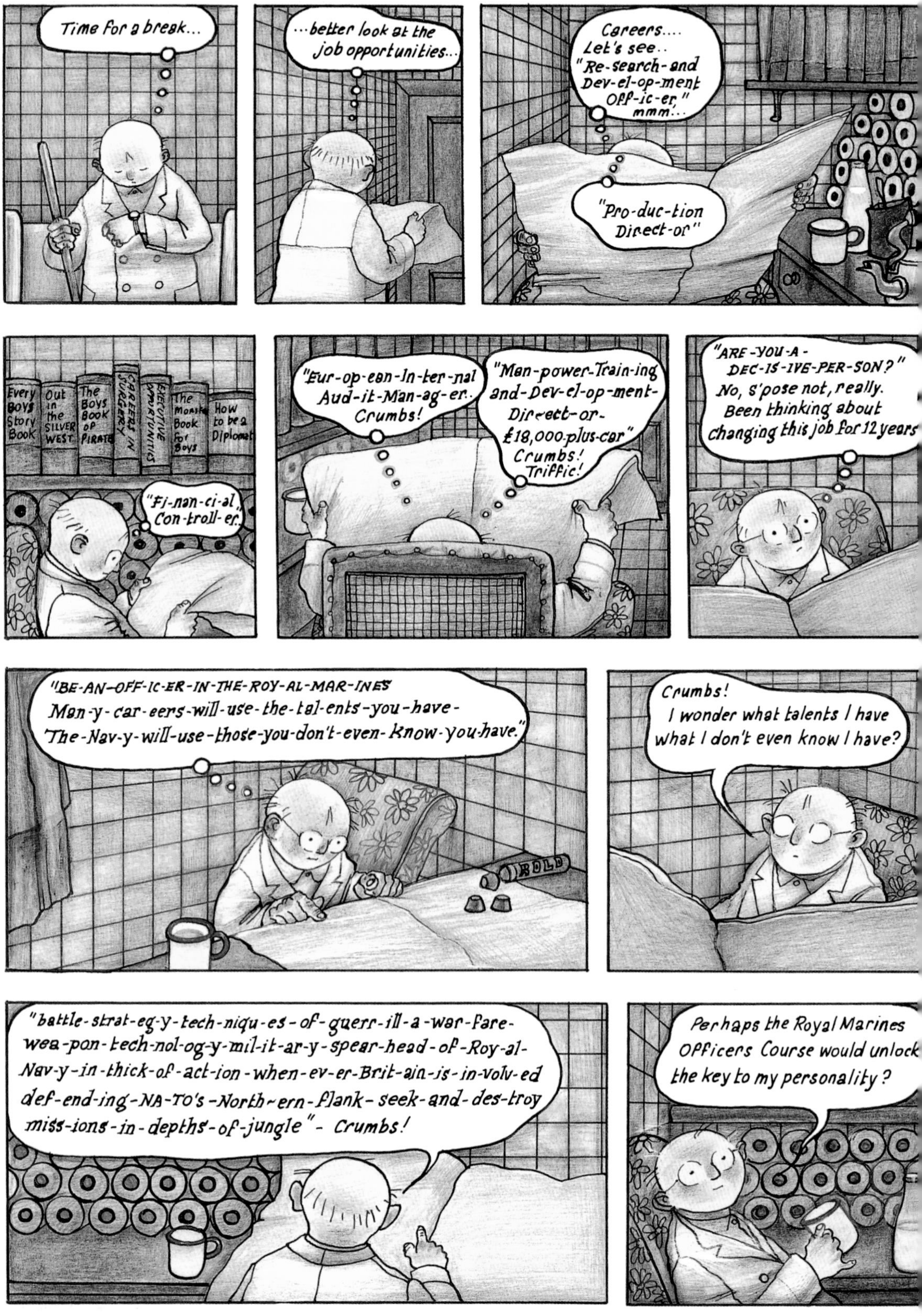

Time for a break...
...better look at the job opportunities...
Careers.... Let's see.. "Re-search-and Dev-el-op-ment Off-ic-er," mmm...
"Pro-duc-tion Direct-or"
Every Boys Story Book
Out in the SILVER WEST
The Boys Book of PIRATES
CAREERS IN SURGERY
EXECUTIVE OPPORTUNITIES
The Monster Book for Boys
How to be a Diplomat
"Fi-nan-ci-al Con-troll-er."
"Eur-op-een-In-ter-nal Aud-it-Man-ag-er. Crumbs!
"Man-power-Train-ing and-Dev-el-op-ment-Direct-or-£18,000-plus-car" Crumbs! Triffic!
"ARE-YOU-A-DEC-IS-IVE-PER-SON?" No, s'pose not, really. Been thinking about changing this job for 12 years
"BE-AN-OFF-IC-ER-IN-THE-ROY-AL-MAR-INES Man-y-car-eers-will-use-the-tal-ents-you-have-The-Nav-y-will-use-those-you-don't-even-know-you-have."
ROLO
Crumbs! I wonder what talents I have what I don't even know I have?
"battle-strat-eg-y-tech-niqu-es-of-guerr-ill-a-war-fare-wea-pon-tech-nol-og-y-mil-it-ar-y-spear-head-of-Roy-al-Nav-y-in-thick-of-act-ion-when-ev-er-Brit-ain-is-in-volv-ed def-end-ing-NA-TO's-North-ern-flank-seek-and-des-troy miss-ions-in-depths-of-jungle" - Crumbs!
Perhaps the Royal Marines Officers Course would unlock the key to my personality?

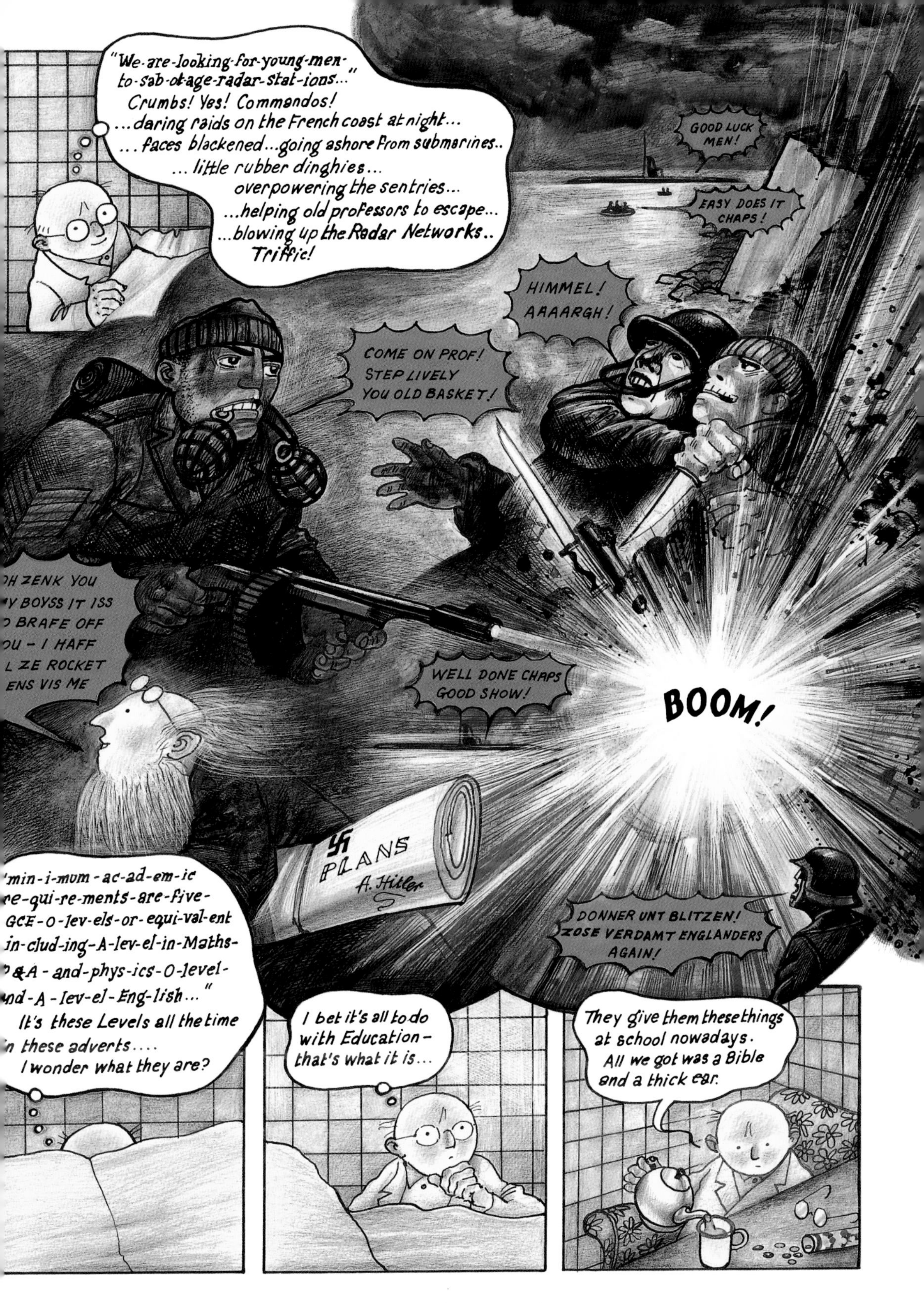
"We-are-looking-for-young-men-to-sab-ot-age-radar-stat-ions..." Crumbs! Yes! Commandos! ...daring raids on the French coast at night... ...faces blackened...going ashore from submarines.. ... little rubber dinghies... overpowering the sentries... ...helping old professors to escape... ...blowing up the Radar Networks.. Triffic!
GOOD LUCK MEN!
EASY DOES IT CHAPS!
COME ON PROF! STEP LIVELY YOU OLD BASKET!
HIMMEL! AAAARGH!
H ZENK YOU Y BOYSS IT ISS BRAFE OFF OU - I HAFF L ZE ROCKET ENS VIS ME
WELL DONE CHAPS GOOD SHOW!
BOOM!
PLANS
A. Hitler
min-i-mum-ac-ad-em-ic re-qui-re-ments-are-five-GCE-O-lev-els-or-equi-val-ent in-clud-ing-A-lev-el-in-Maths-&A-and-phys-ics-O-level-nd-A-lev-el-Eng-lish..." It's these Levels all the time n these adverts.... I wonder what they are?
DONNER UNT BLITZEN! ZOSE VERDAMT ENGLANDERS AGAIN!
I bet it's all to do with Education - that's what it is...
They give them these things at school nowadays. All we got was a Bible and a thick ear.

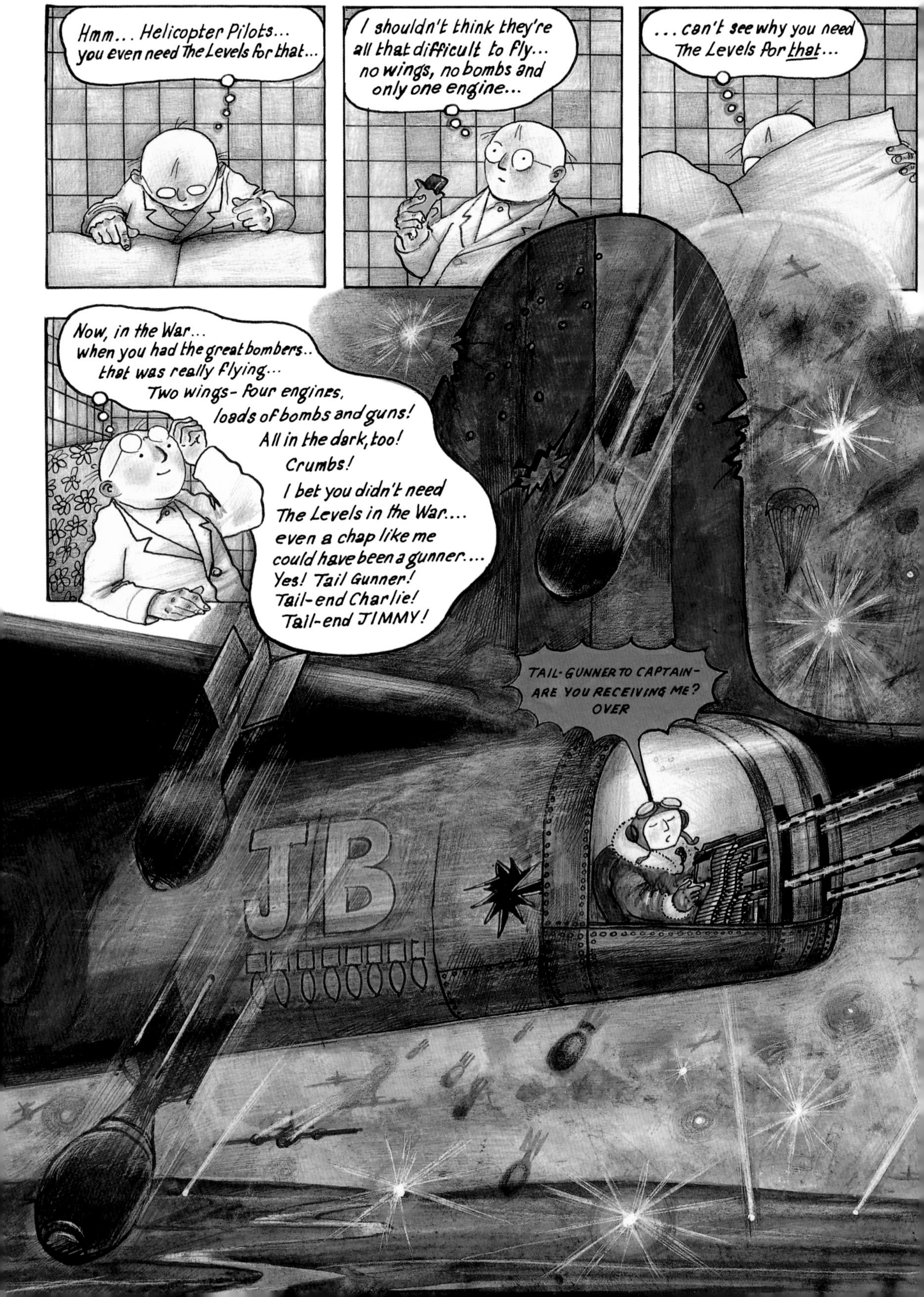
Hmm... Helicopter Pilots... you even need The Levels for that...
I shouldn't think they're all that difficult to fly... no wings, no bombs and only one engine...
...can't see why you need The Levels for that...
Now, in the War... when you had the great bombers.. that was really flying... Two wings- four engines, loads of bombs and guns! All in the dark, too! Crumbs! I bet you didn't need The Levels in the War.... even a chap like me could have been a gunner.... Yes! Tail Gunner! Tail-end Charlie! Tail-end JIMMY!
TAIL-GUNNER TO CAPTAIN- ARE YOU RECEIVING ME? OVER
JB

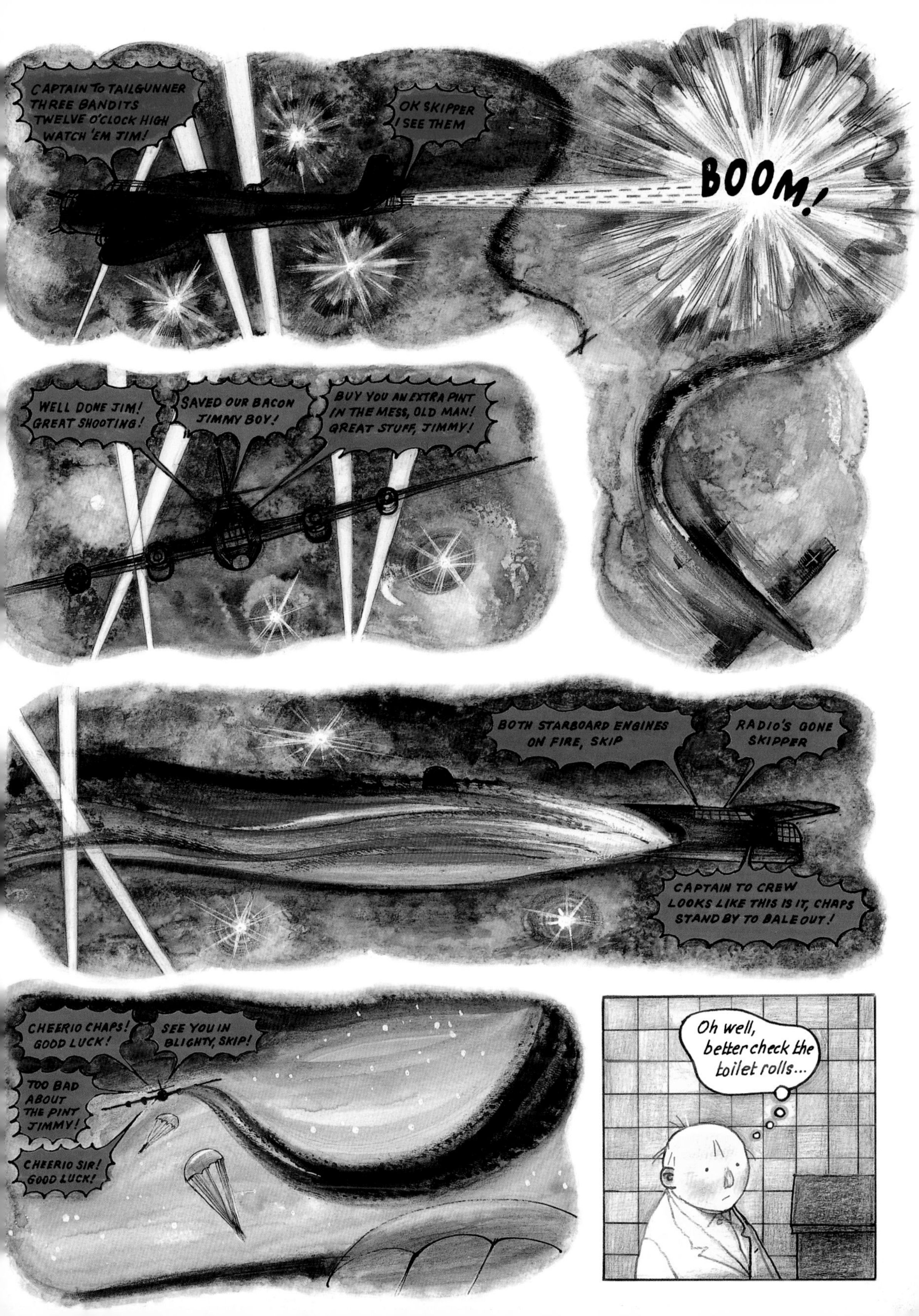
CAPTAIN TO TAILGUNNER THREE BANDITS TWELVE O'CLOCK HIGH WATCH 'EM JIM!
OK SKIPPER I SEE THEM
BOOM!
WELL DONE JIM! GREAT SHOOTING!
SAVED OUR BACON JIMMY BOY!
BUY YOU AN EXTRA PINT IN THE MESS, OLD MAN! GREAT STUFF, JIMMY!
BOTH STARBOARD ENGINES ON FIRE, SKIP
RADIO'S GONE SKIPPER
CAPTAIN TO CREW LOOKS LIKE THIS IS IT, CHAPS STAND BY TO BALE OUT!
CHEERIO CHAPS! GOOD LUCK!
SEE YOU IN BLIGHTY, SKIP!
TOO BAD ABOUT THE PINT JIMMY!
CHEERIO SIR! GOOD LUCK!
Oh well, better check the toilet rolls...

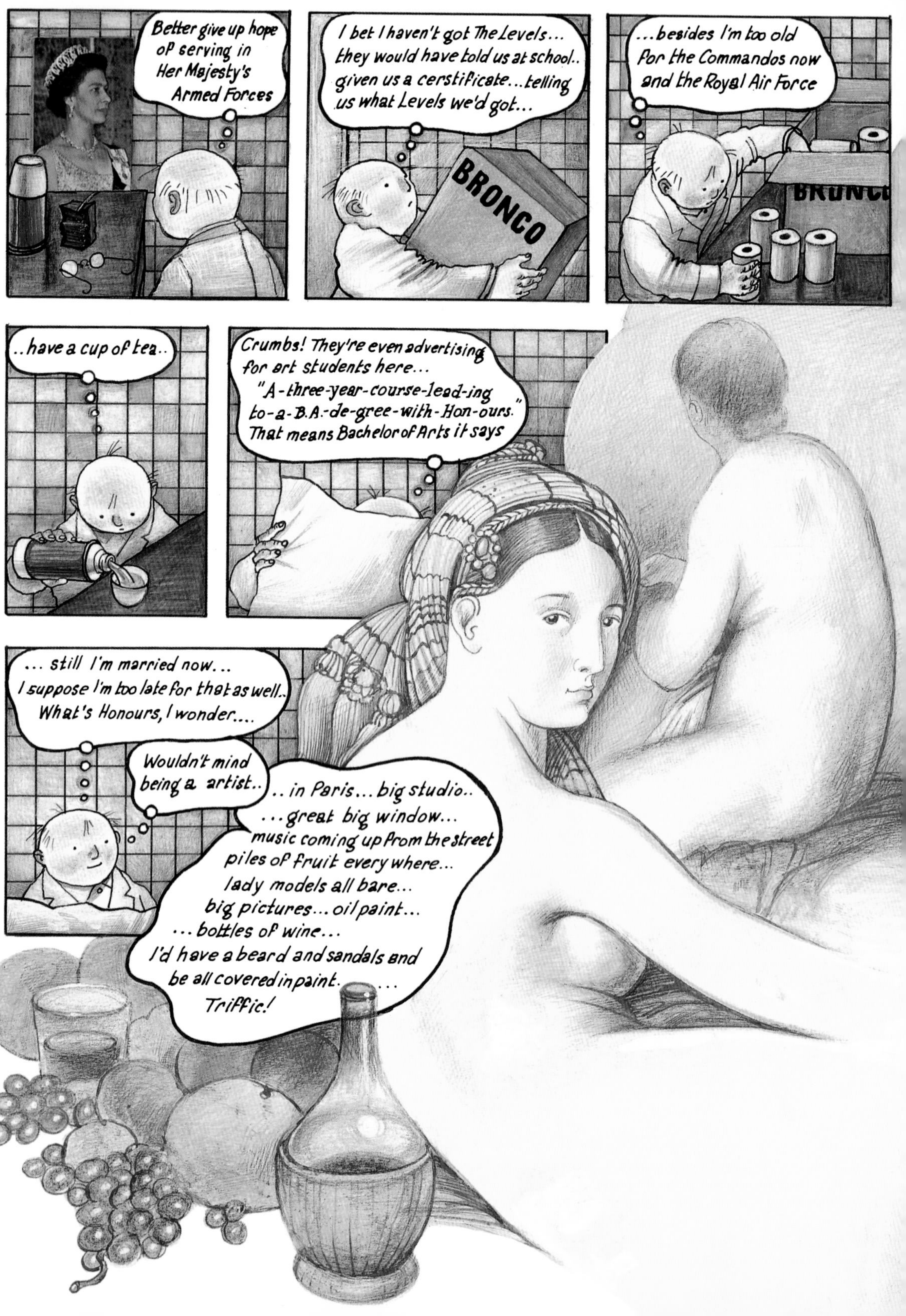
Better give up hope of serving in Her Majesty's Armed Forces
I bet I haven't got The Levels... they would have told us at school.. given us a cerstificate...telling us what Levels we'd got...
BRONCO
...besides I'm too old for the Commandos now and the Royal Air Force
..have a cup of tea..
Crumbs! They're even advertising for art students here... "A-three-year-course-lead-ing to-a-B.A.-de-gree-with-Hon-ours." That means Bachelor of Arts it says
... still I'm married now... I suppose I'm too late for that as well.. What's Honours, I wonder....
Wouldn't mind being a artist..
.. in Paris... big studio.. ...great big window... music coming up from the street piles of fruit every where... lady models all bare... big pictures... oil paint... ...bottles of wine... I'd have a beard and sandals and be all covered in paint. ... Triffic!

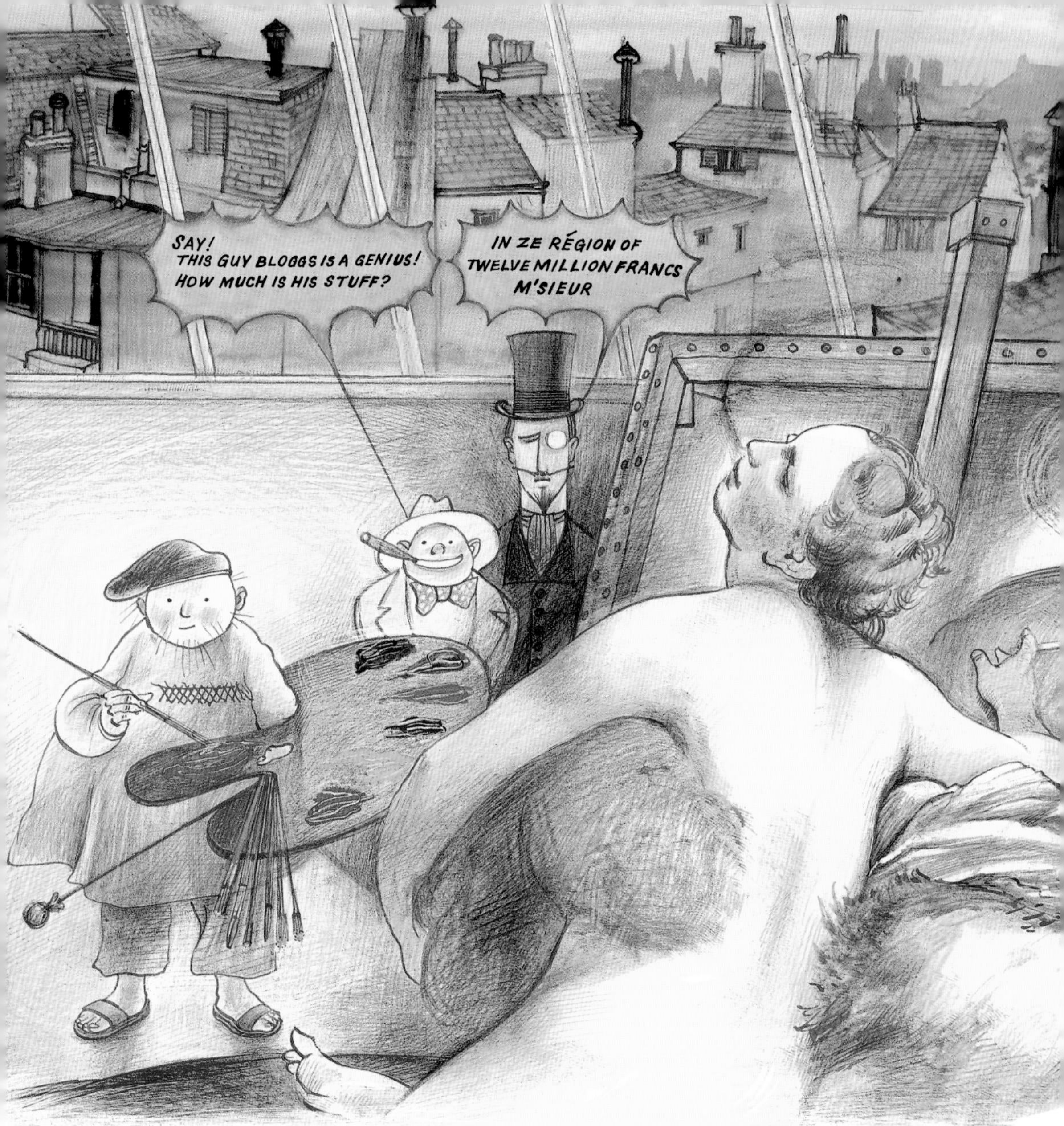
SAY!
THIS GUY BLOGGS IS A GENIUS!
HOW MUCH IS HIS STUFF?
IN ZE RÉGION OF
TWELVE MILLION FRANCS
M'SIEUR

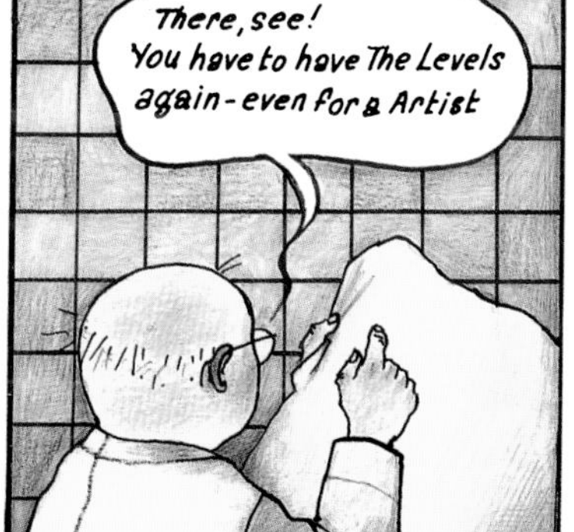
There, see!
You have to have The Levels
again - even for a Artist

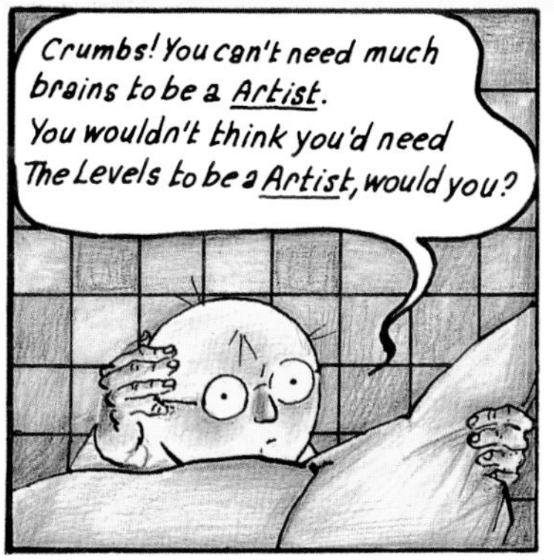
Crumbs! You can't need much
brains to be a Artist.
You wouldn't think you'd need
The Levels to be a Artist, would you?

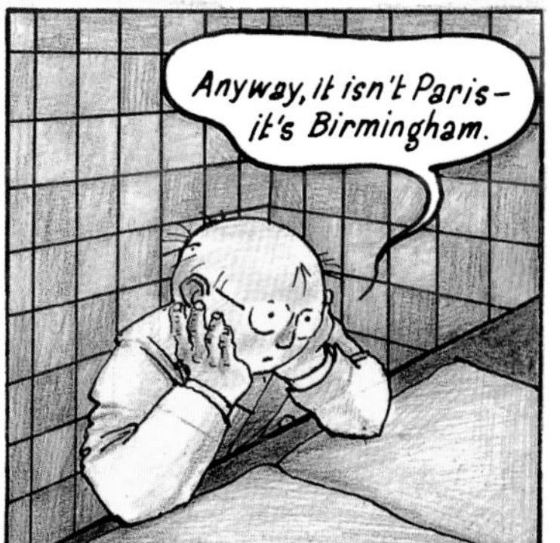
Anyway, it isn't Paris -
it's Birmingham.

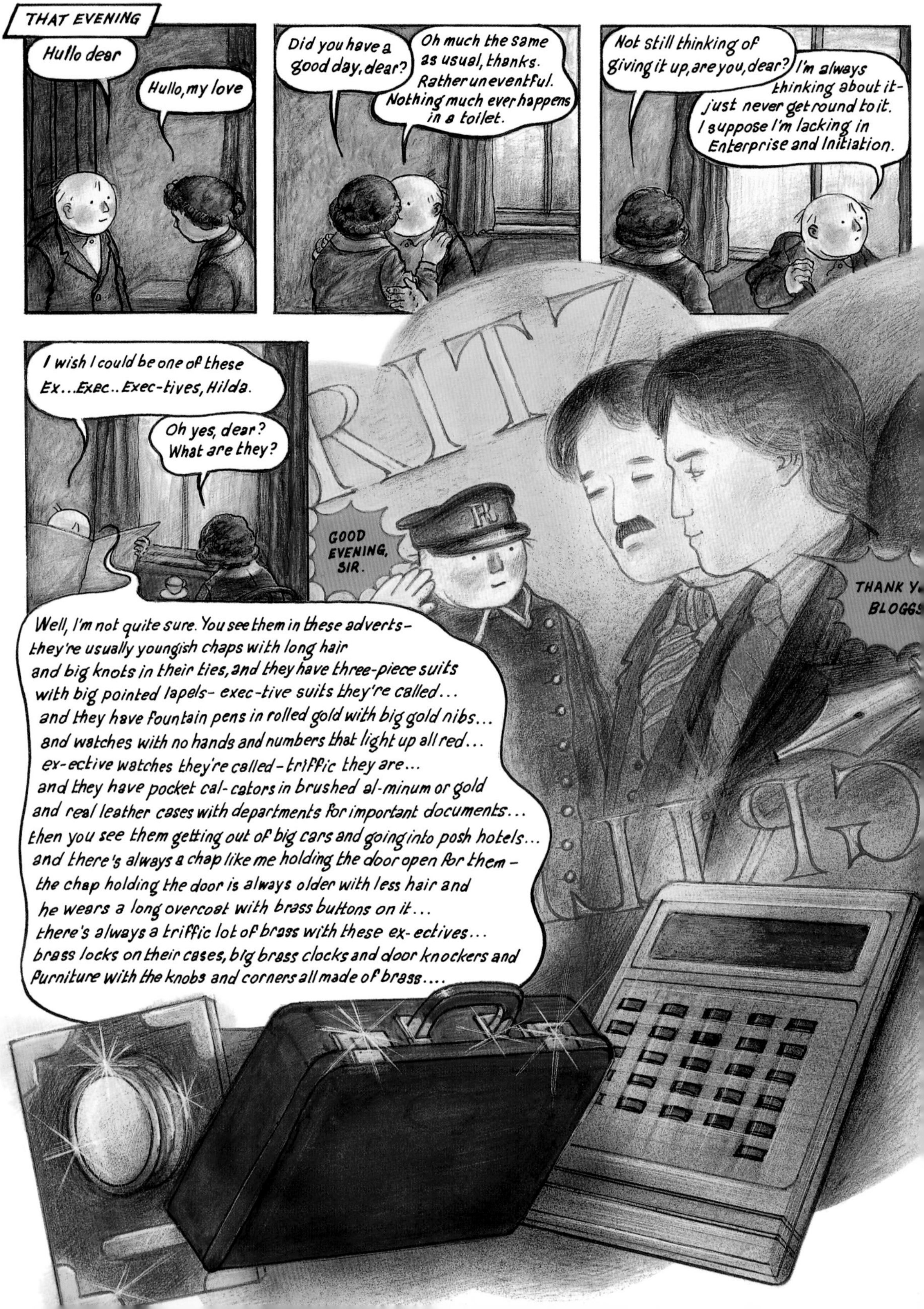
THAT EVENING
Hullo dear
Hullo, my love
Did you have a good day, dear?
Oh much the same as usual, thanks. Rather uneventful. Nothing much ever happens in a toilet.
Not still thinking of giving it up, are you, dear?
I'm always thinking about it - just never get round to it. I suppose I'm lacking in Enterprise and Initiation.
I wish I could be one of these Ex...Exec..Exec-tives, Hilda.
Oh yes, dear? What are they?
Well, I'm not quite sure. You see them in these adverts - they're usually youngish chaps with long hair and big knots in their ties, and they have three-piece suits with big pointed lapels - exec-tive suits they're called... and they have fountain pens in rolled gold with big gold nibs... and watches with no hands and numbers that light up all red... ex-ective watches they're called - triffic they are... and they have pocket cal-cators in brushed al-minum or gold and real leather cases with departments for important documents... then you see them getting out of big cars and going into posh hotels... and there's always a chap like me holding the door open for them - the chap holding the door is always older with less hair and he wears a long overcoat with brass buttons on it... there's always a triffic lot of brass with these ex-ectives... brass locks on their cases, big brass clocks and door knockers and furniture with the knobs and corners all made of brass....
GOOD EVENING, SIR.
THANK Y
BLOGGS
RITZ

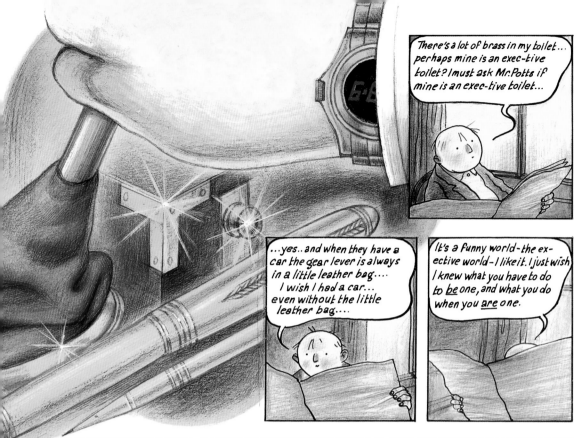

There's a lot of brass in my toilet... perhaps mine is an exec-tive toilet? I must ask Mr. Potts if mine is an exec-tive toilet...

...yes.. and when they have a car the gear lever is always in a little leather bag.... I wish I had a car... even without the little leather bag....

It's a funny world - the ex-ective world - I like it. I just wish I knew what you have to do to be one, and what you do when you are one.

LATER I expect it's like all these interesting jobs, Hilda. You have to have The Levels to get started.

Oh? What's the levels, dear?

I'm not sure, I think they give you them at school, nowadays.

I see, dear

They didn't give you any Levels did they, Hilda?

No, I don't think so, dear, They gave me a nice book, though.

Oh, what was it?

Prayers

Oh

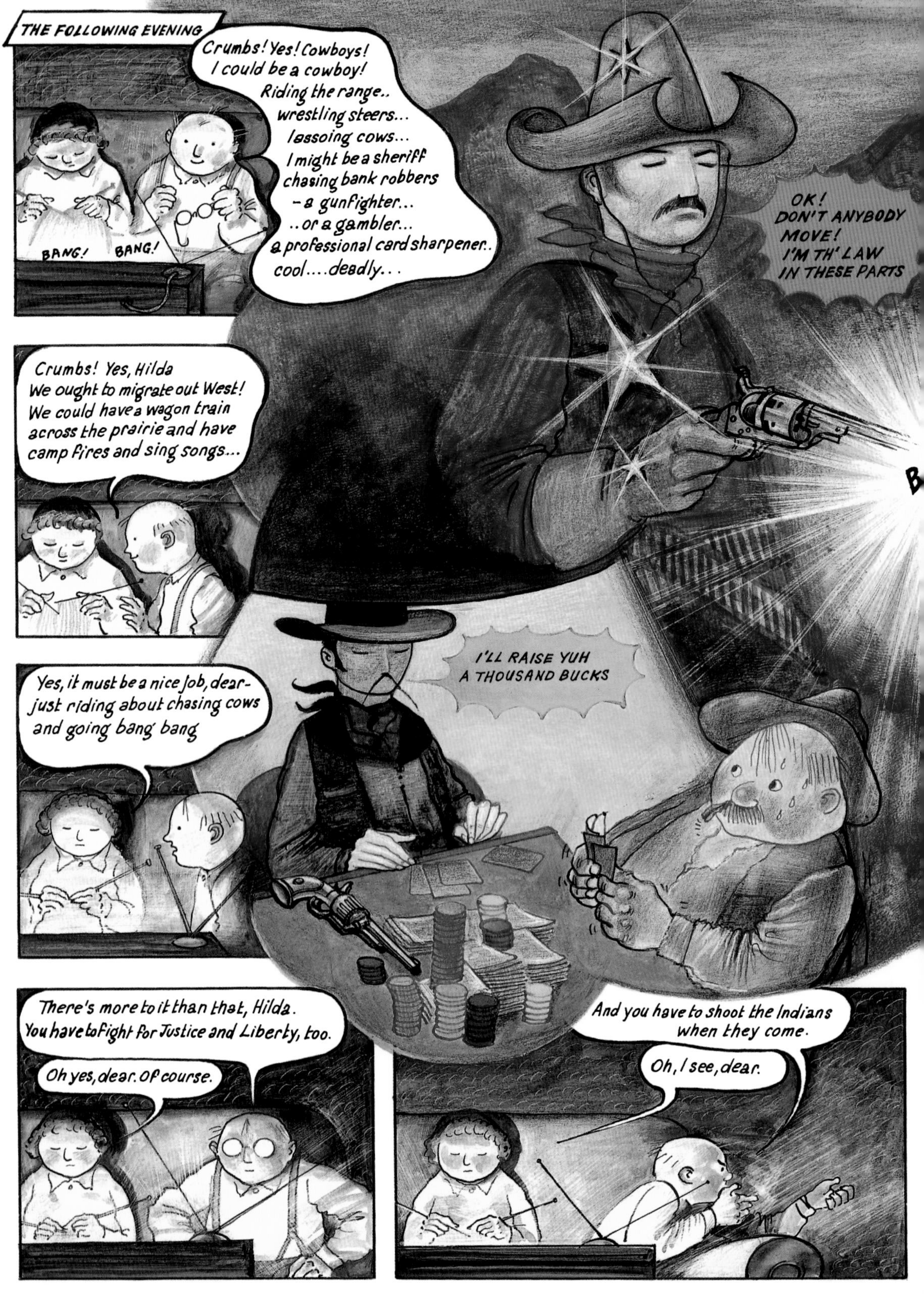
THE FOLLOWING EVENING
Crumbs! Yes! Cowboys! I could be a cowboy! Riding the range.. wrestling steers... lassoing cows... I might be a sheriff chasing bank robbers – a gunfighter... ..or a gambler... a professional card sharpener.. cool....deadly...
BANG! BANG!
OK! DON'T ANYBODY MOVE! I'M TH' LAW IN THESE PARTS
Crumbs! Yes, Hilda We ought to migrate out West! We could have a wagon train across the prairie and have camp fires and sing songs...
I'LL RAISE YUH A THOUSAND BUCKS
Yes, it must be a nice job, dear- just riding about chasing cows and going bang bang
There's more to it than that, Hilda. You have to fight for Justice and Liberty, too.
Oh yes, dear. Of course.
And you have to shoot the Indians when they come.
Oh, I see, dear.

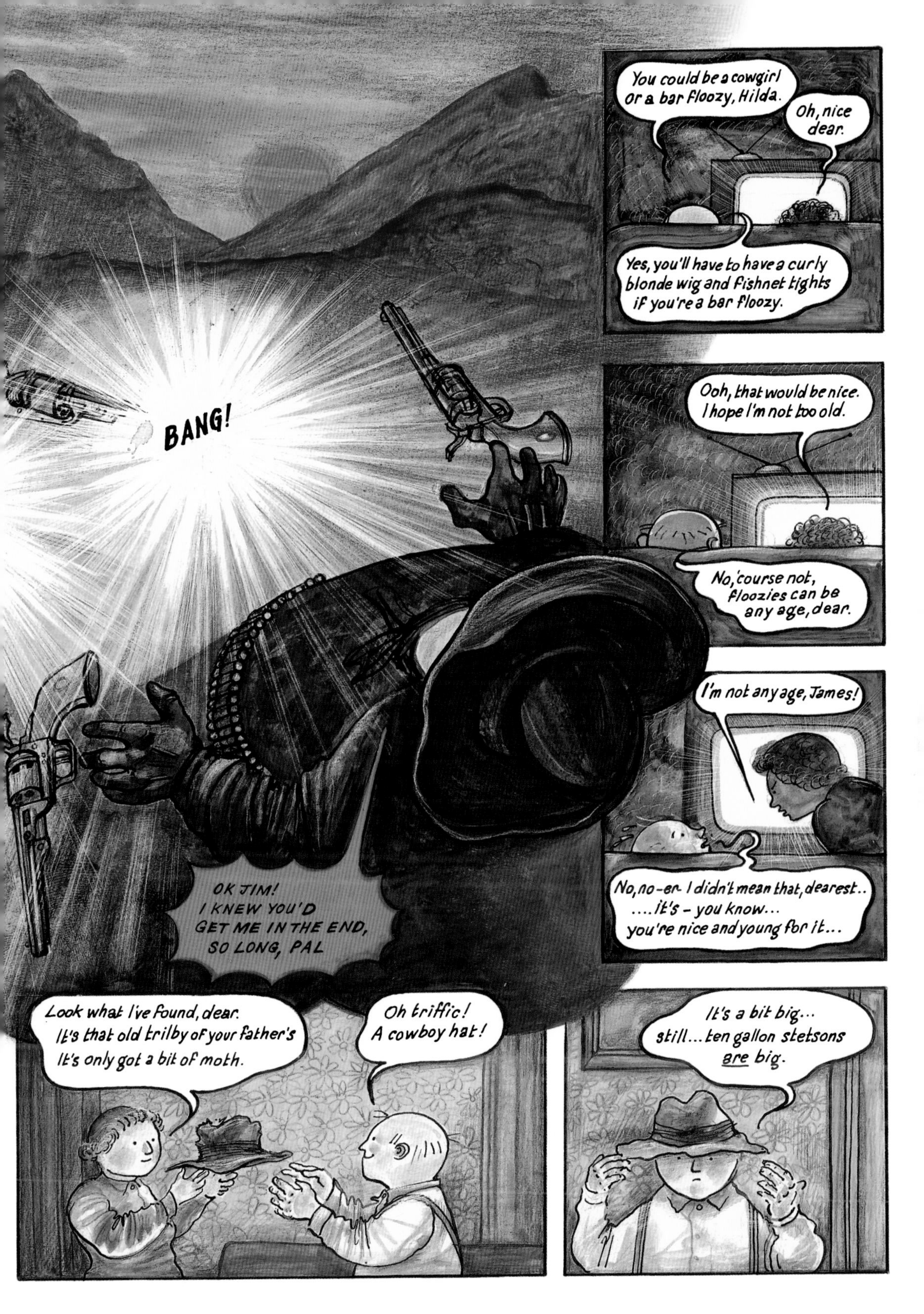

You could be a cowgirl or a bar floozy, Hilda.
Oh, nice dear.
Yes, you'll have to have a curly blonde wig and fishnet tights if you're a bar floozy.
BANG!
Ooh, that would be nice. I hope I'm not too old.
No, 'course not, floozies can be any age, dear.
I'm not any age, James!
No, no - er- I didn't mean that, dearest.. ....it's - you know... you're nice and young for it...
OK JIM! I KNEW YOU'D GET ME IN THE END, SO LONG, PAL
Look what I've found, dear. It's that old trilby of your father's It's only got a bit of moth.
Oh triffic! A cowboy hat!
It's a bit big... still... ten gallon stetsons are big.

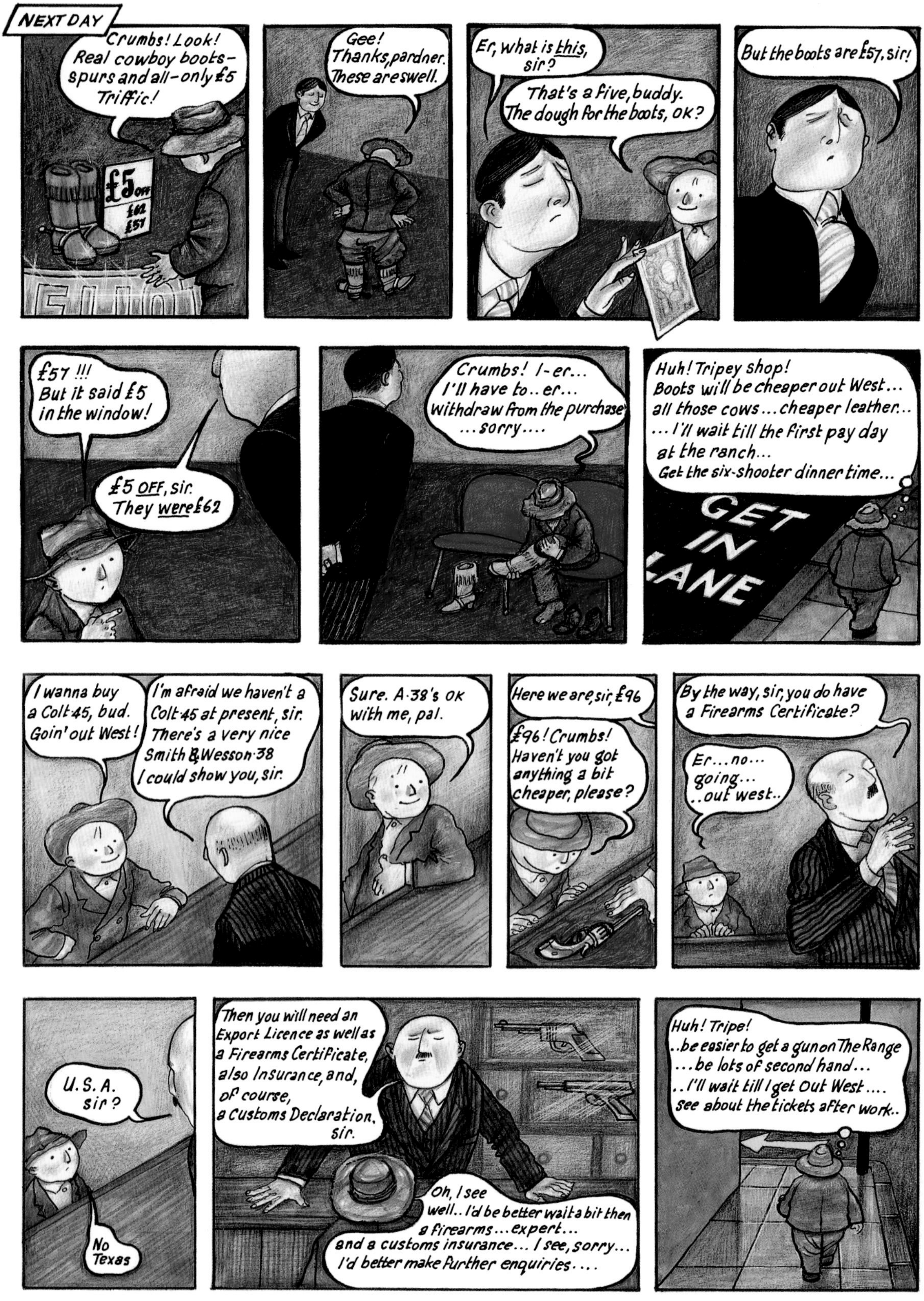
NEXT DAY
Crumbs! Look! Real cowboy boots - spurs and all - only £5 Triffic!
£5 OFF
£62
£57
Gee! Thanks, pardner. These are swell.
Er, what is this, sir?
That's a five, buddy. The dough for the boots, OK?
But the boots are £57, sir!
£57 !!! But it said £5 in the window!
£5 OFF, sir. They were £62
Crumbs! I-er... I'll have to.. er... withdraw from the purchase ...sorry....
Huh! Tripey shop! Boots will be cheaper out West... all those cows... cheaper leather... ...I'll wait till the first pay day at the ranch... Get the six-shooter dinner time...
GET IN LANE
I wanna buy a Colt·45, bud. Goin' out West!
I'm afraid we haven't a Colt·45 at present, sir. There's a very nice Smith & Wesson·38 I could show you, sir.
Sure. A·38's OK with me, pal.
Here we are, sir, £96
£96! Crumbs! Haven't you got anything a bit cheaper, please?
By the way, sir, you do have a Firearms Certificate?
Er...no... going... ..out west..
U.S.A. sir?
No Texas
Then you will need an Export Licence as well as a Firearms Certificate, also Insurance, and, of course, a Customs Declaration, sir.
Oh, I see well.. I'd be better wait a bit then a firearms...expert... and a customs insurance... I see, sorry... I'd better make further enquiries....
Huh! Tripe! ..be easier to get a gun on The Range ...be lots of second hand... ..I'll wait till I get Out West.... see about the tickets after work..

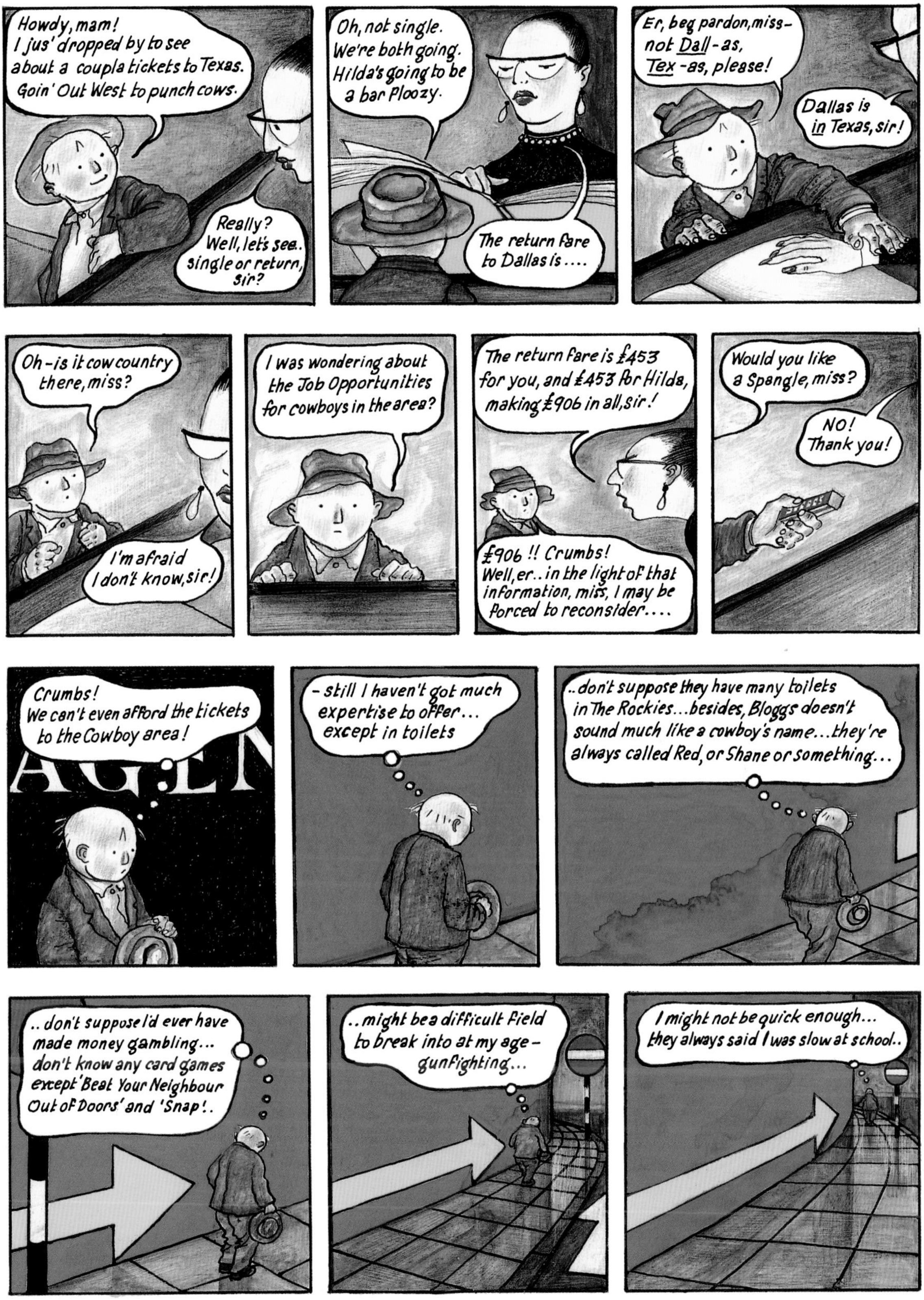

Howdy, mam! I jus' dropped by to see about a coupla tickets to Texas. Goin' Out West to punch cows.
Really? Well, let's see.. single or return, sir?
Oh, not single. We're both going. Hilda's going to be a bar Floozy.
The return fare to Dallas is ....
Er, beg pardon, miss - not Dall-as, Tex-as, please!
Dallas is in Texas, sir!
Oh - is it cow country there, miss?
I'm afraid I don't know, sir!
I was wondering about the Job Opportunities for cowboys in the area?
The return fare is £453 for you, and £453 for Hilda, making £906 in all, sir!
£906 !! Crumbs! Well, er.. in the light of that information, miss, I may be forced to reconsider....
Would you like a Spangle, miss?
NO! Thank you!
Crumbs! We can't even afford the tickets to the Cowboy area!
AGEN
- still I haven't got much expertise to offer... except in toilets
..don't suppose they have many toilets in The Rockies...besides, Bloggs doesn't sound much like a cowboy's name...they're always called Red, or Shane or something...
.. don't suppose I'd ever have made money gambling... don't know any card games except 'Beat Your Neighbour Out of Doors' and 'Snap'!..
..might be a difficult field to break into at my age - gunfighting...
I might not be quick enough... they always said I was slow at school..

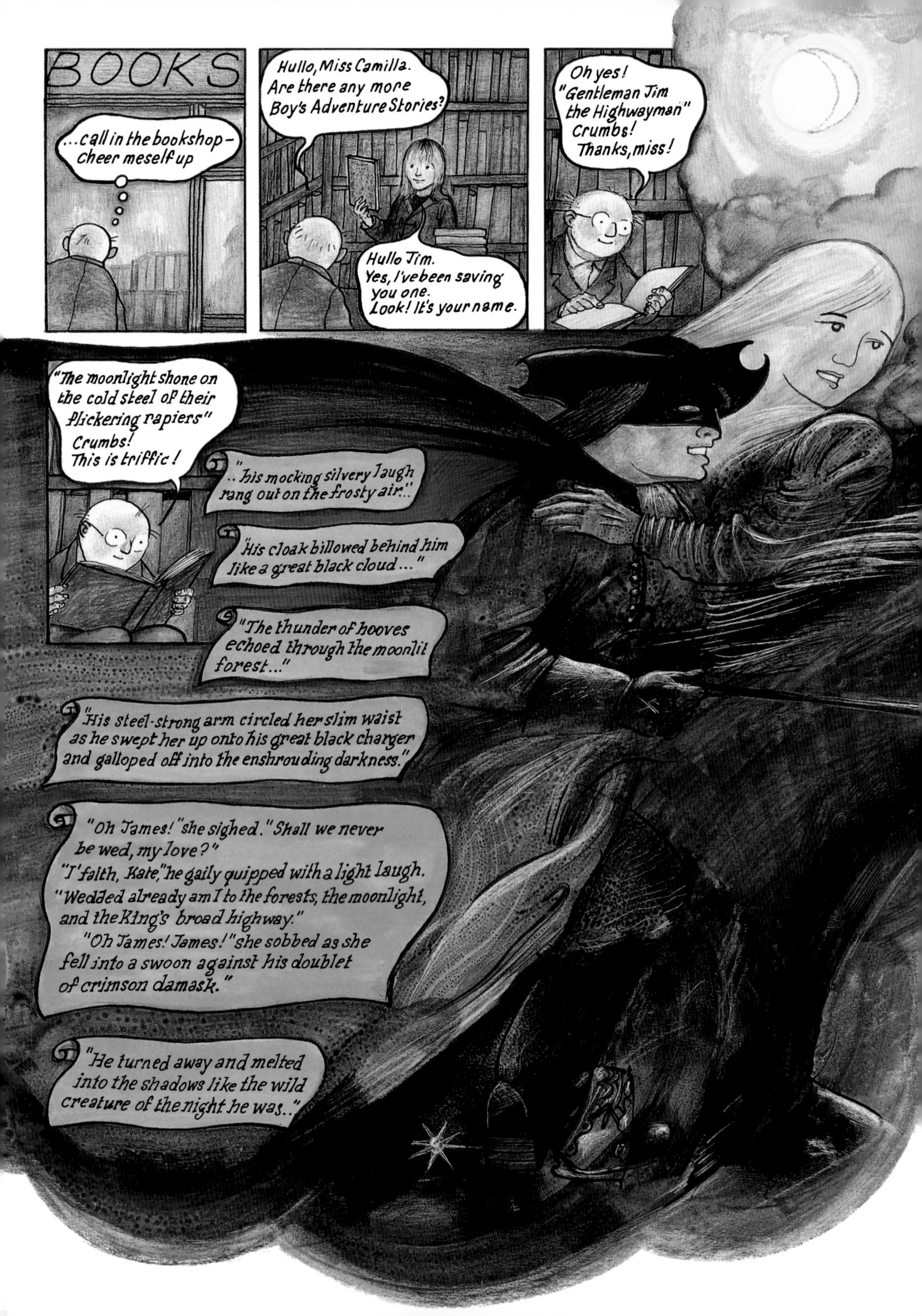

BOOKS
...call in the bookshop - cheer meself up
Hullo, Miss Camilla. Are there any more Boy's Adventure Stories?
Hullo Jim. Yes, I've been saving you one. Look! It's your name.
Oh yes! "Gentleman Jim the Highwayman" Crumbs! Thanks, miss!
"The moonlight shone on the cold steel of their flickering rapiers" Crumbs! This is triffic!
"..his mocking silvery laugh rang out on the frosty air.."
"His cloak billowed behind him like a great black cloud..."
"The thunder of hooves echoed through the moonlit forest..."
"His steel-strong arm circled her slim waist as he swept her up onto his great black charger and galloped off into the enshrouding darkness."
"Oh James!" she sighed. "Shall we never be wed, my love?" "I'faith, Kate," he gaily quipped with a light laugh. "Wedded already am I to the forests, the moonlight, and the King's broad highway." "Oh James! James!" she sobbed as she fell into a swoon against his doublet of crimson damask."
"He turned away and melted into the shadows like the wild creature of the night he was.."

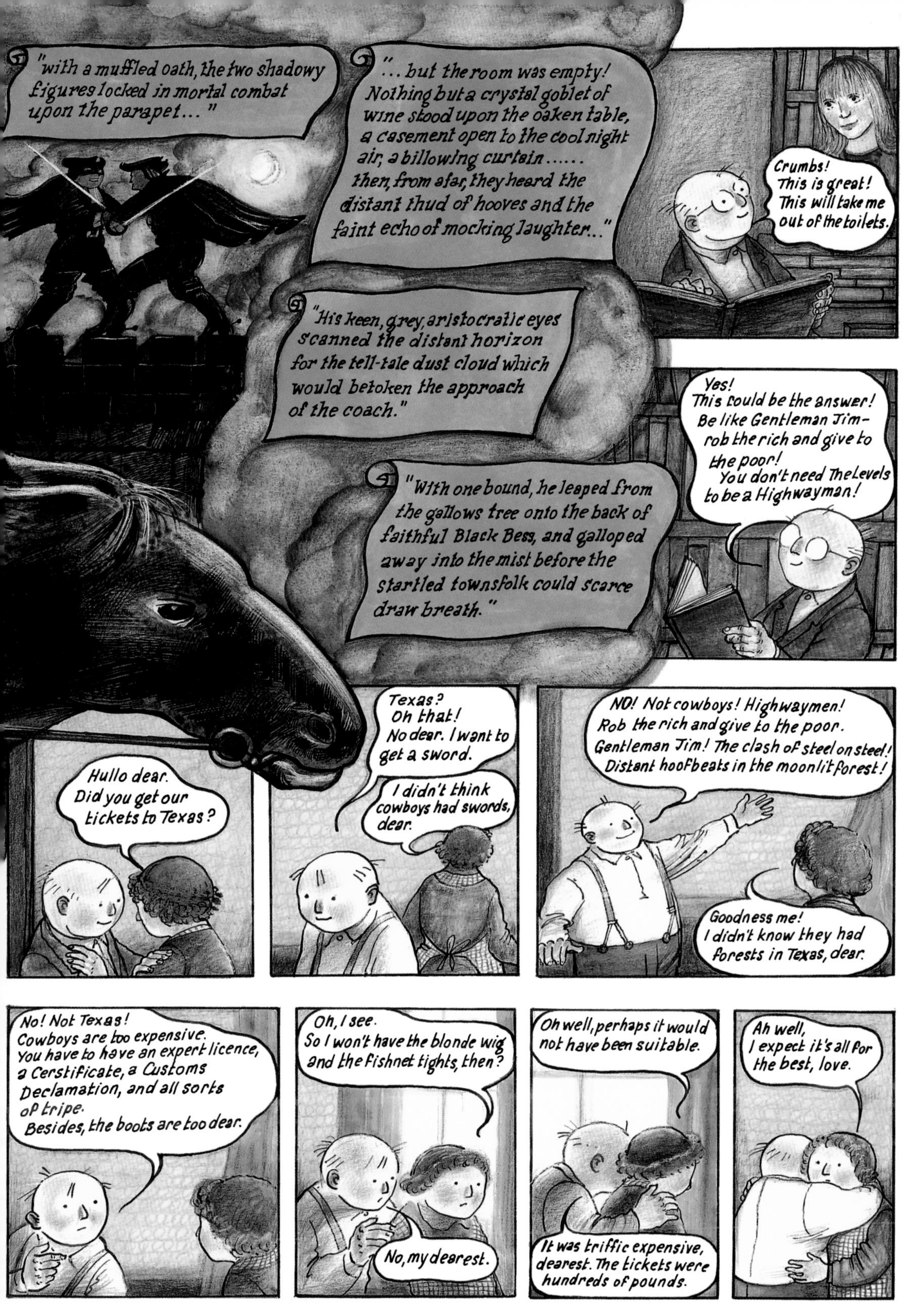
"with a muffled oath, the two shadowy figures locked in mortal combat upon the parapet..."
"... but the room was empty! Nothing but a crystal goblet of wine stood upon the oaken table, a casement open to the cool night air, a billowing curtain...... then, from afar, they heard the distant thud of hooves and the faint echo of mocking laughter.."
Crumbs! This is great! This will take me out of the toilets.
"His keen, grey, aristocratic eyes scanned the distant horizon for the tell-tale dust cloud which would betoken the approach of the coach."
"With one bound, he leaped from the gallows tree onto the back of faithful Black Bess, and galloped away into the mist before the startled townsfolk could scarce draw breath."
Yes! This could be the answer! Be like Gentleman Jim – rob the rich and give to the poor! You don't need The Levels to be a Highwayman!
Hullo dear. Did you get our tickets to Texas?
Texas? Oh that! No dear. I want to get a sword.
I didn't think cowboys had swords, dear.
NO! Not cowboys! Highwaymen! Rob the rich and give to the poor. Gentleman Jim! The clash of steel on steel! Distant hoofbeats in the moonlit forest!
Goodness me! I didn't know they had forests in Texas, dear.
No! Not Texas! Cowboys are too expensive. You have to have an expert licence, a Cerstificate, a Customs Declamation, and all sorts of tripe. Besides, the boots are too dear.
Oh, I see. So I won't have the blonde wig and the fishnet tights, then?
No, my dearest.
Oh well, perhaps it would not have been suitable.
It was triffic expensive, dearest. The tickets were hundreds of pounds.
Ah well, I expect it's all for the best, love.

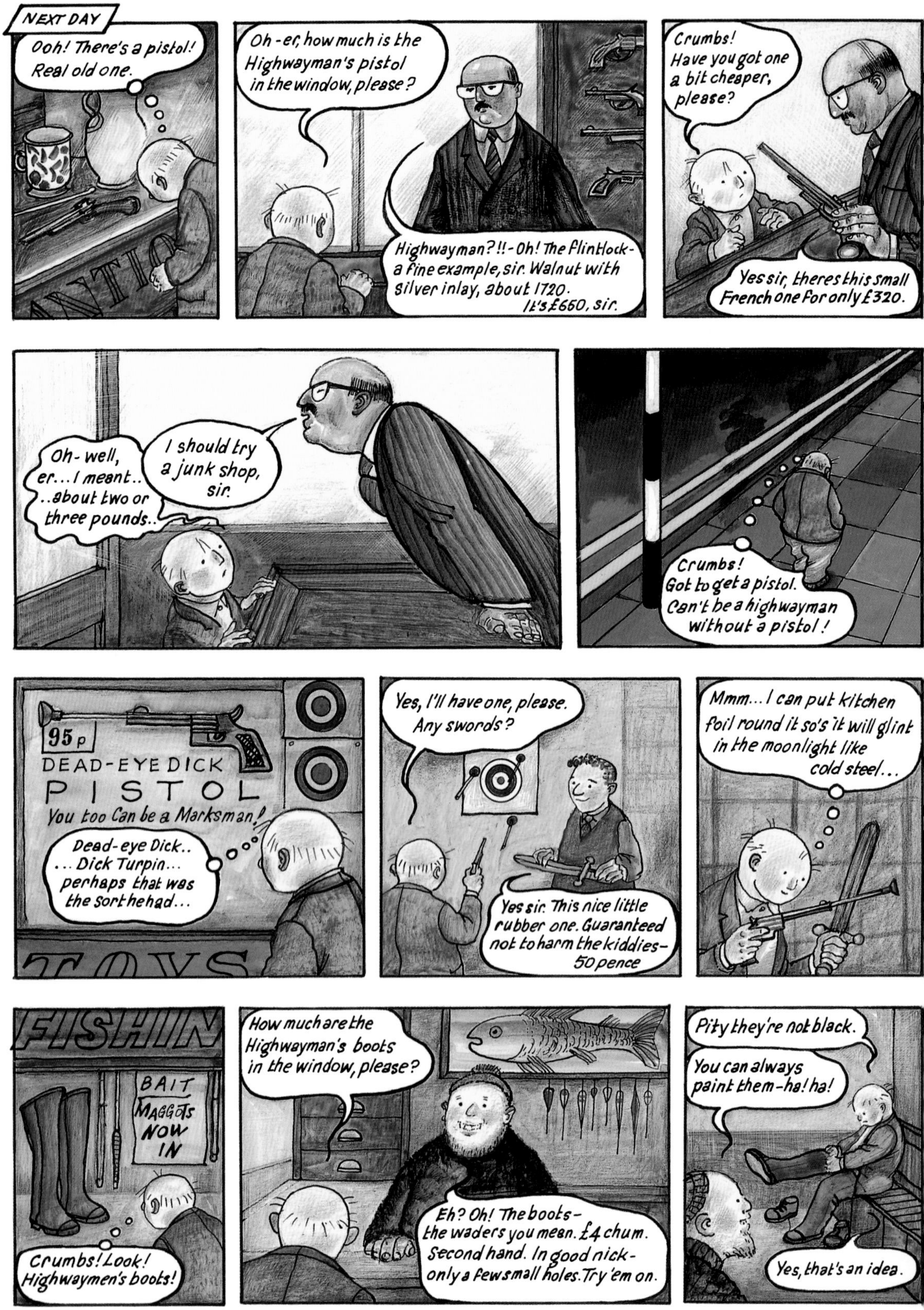
NEXT DAY
Ooh! There's a pistol! Real old one.
ANTIQ
Oh-er, how much is the Highwayman's pistol in the window, please?
Highwayman?!!-Oh! The flintlock- a fine example, sir. Walnut with silver inlay, about 1720. It's £650, sir.
Crumbs! Have you got one a bit cheaper, please?
Yes sir, theres this small French one for only £320.
Oh-well, er... I meant.. ..about two or three pounds..
I should try a junk shop, sir.
Crumbs! Got to get a pistol. Can't be a highwayman without a pistol!
95p
DEAD-EYE DICK PISTOL
You too Can be a Marksman!
Dead-eye Dick.. ...Dick Turpin... perhaps that was the sort he had...
TOYS
Yes, I'll have one, please. Any swords?
Yes sir. This nice little rubber one. Guaranteed not to harm the kiddies- 50 pence
Mmm... I can put kitchen foil round it so's it will glint in the moonlight like cold steel...
FISHIN
BAIT
MAGGOTS NOW IN
Crumbs! Look! Highwaymen's boots!
How much are the Highwayman's boots in the window, please?
Eh? Oh! The boots- the waders you mean. £4 chum. Second hand. In good nick- only a few small holes. Try 'em on.
Pity they're not black.
You can always paint them-ha! ha!
Yes, that's an idea.

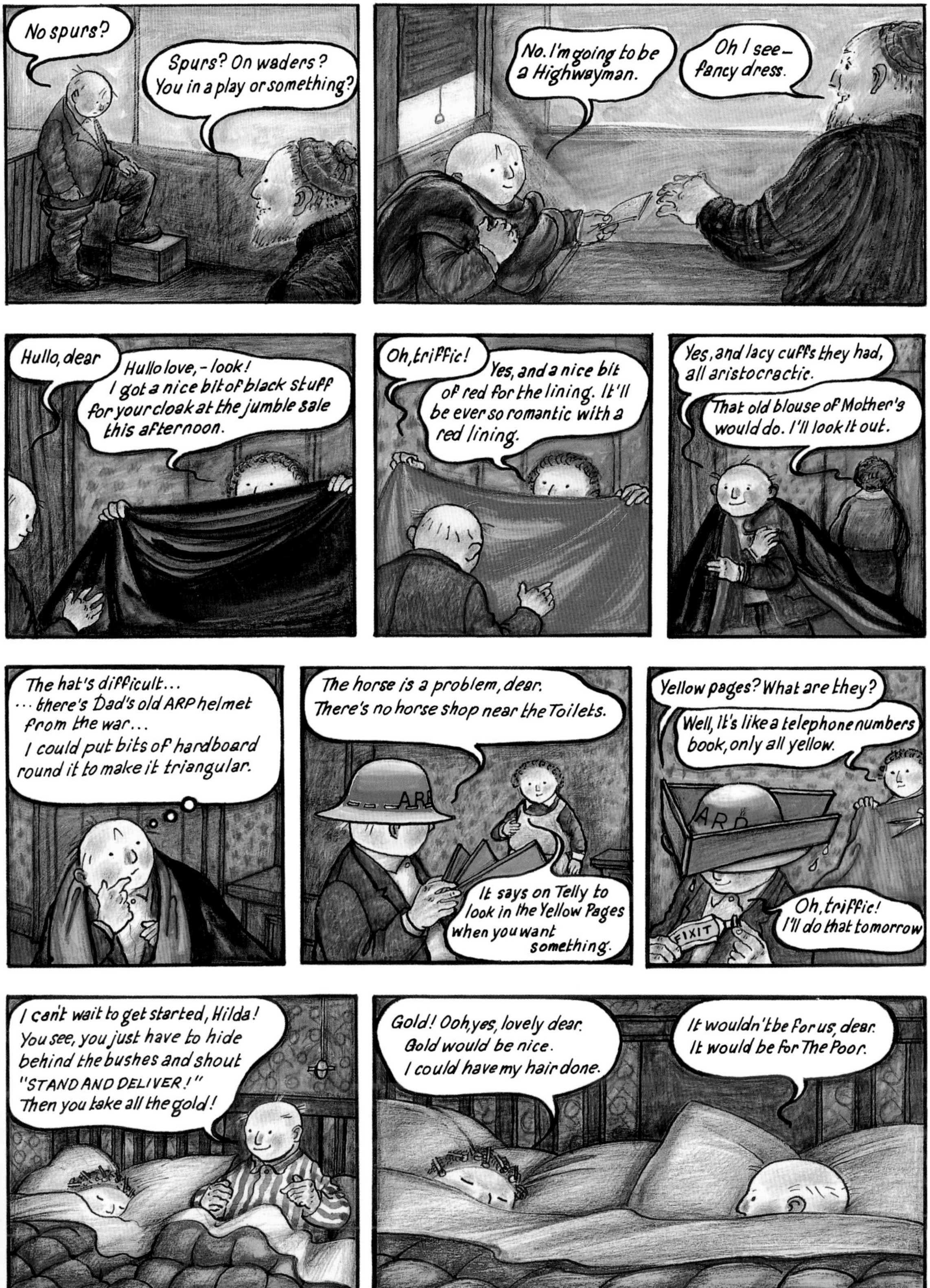
No spurs?
Spurs? On waders? You in a play or something?
No. I'm going to be a Highwayman.
Oh I see – fancy dress.
Hullo, dear
Hullo love, – look! I got a nice bit of black stuff for your cloak at the jumble sale this afternoon.
Oh, triffic!
Yes, and a nice bit of red for the lining. It'll be ever so romantic with a red lining.
Yes, and lacy cuffs they had, all aristocractic.
That old blouse of Mother's would do. I'll look it out.
The hat's difficult... ... there's Dad's old ARP helmet from the war... I could put bits of hardboard round it to make it triangular.
The horse is a problem, dear. There's no horse shop near the Toilets.
ARP
It says on Telly to look in the Yellow Pages when you want something.
Yellow pages? What are they?
Well, it's like a telephone numbers book, only all yellow.
ARP
FIXIT
Oh, triffic! I'll do that tomorrow
I can't wait to get started, Hilda! You see, you just have to hide behind the bushes and shout "STAND AND DELIVER!" Then you take all the gold!
Gold! Ooh, yes, lovely dear. Gold would be nice. I could have my hair done.
It wouldn't be for us, dear. It would be for The Poor.

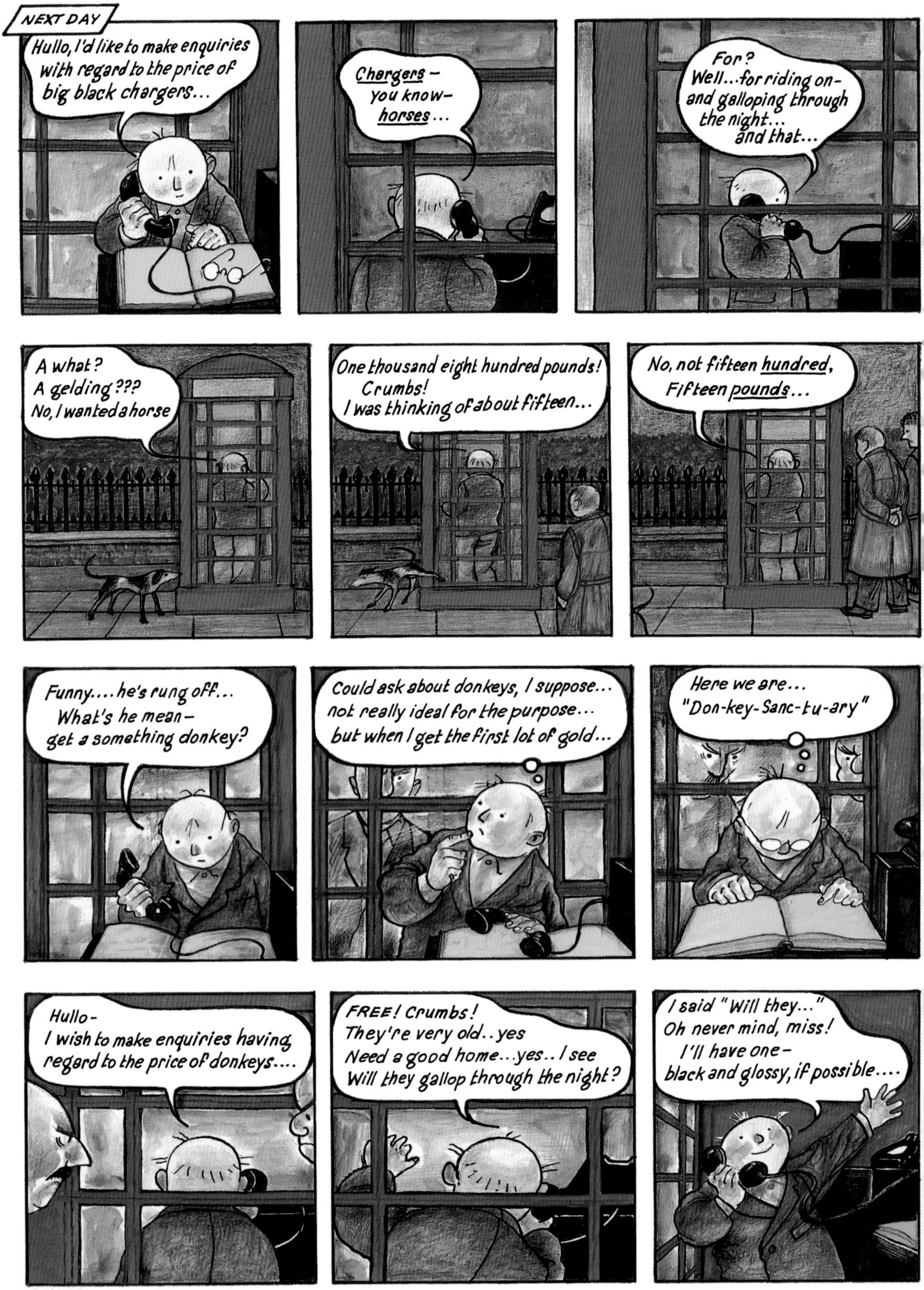
NEXT DAY
Hullo, I'd like to make enquiries with regard to the price of big black chargers...
Chargers - you know - horses...
For? Well...for riding on - and galloping through the night... and that...
A what? A gelding??? No, I wanted a horse
One thousand eight hundred pounds! Crumbs! I was thinking of about fifteen...
No, not fifteen hundred, Fifteen pounds...
Funny.... he's rung off... What's he mean - get a something donkey?
Could ask about donkeys, I suppose... not really ideal for the purpose... but when I get the first lot of gold...
Here we are... "Don-key-Sanc-tu-ary"
Hullo - I wish to make enquiries having regard to the price of donkeys....
FREE! Crumbs! They're very old..yes Need a good home...yes..I see Will they gallop through the night?
I said "Will they..." Oh never mind, miss! I'll have one - black and glossy, if possible....

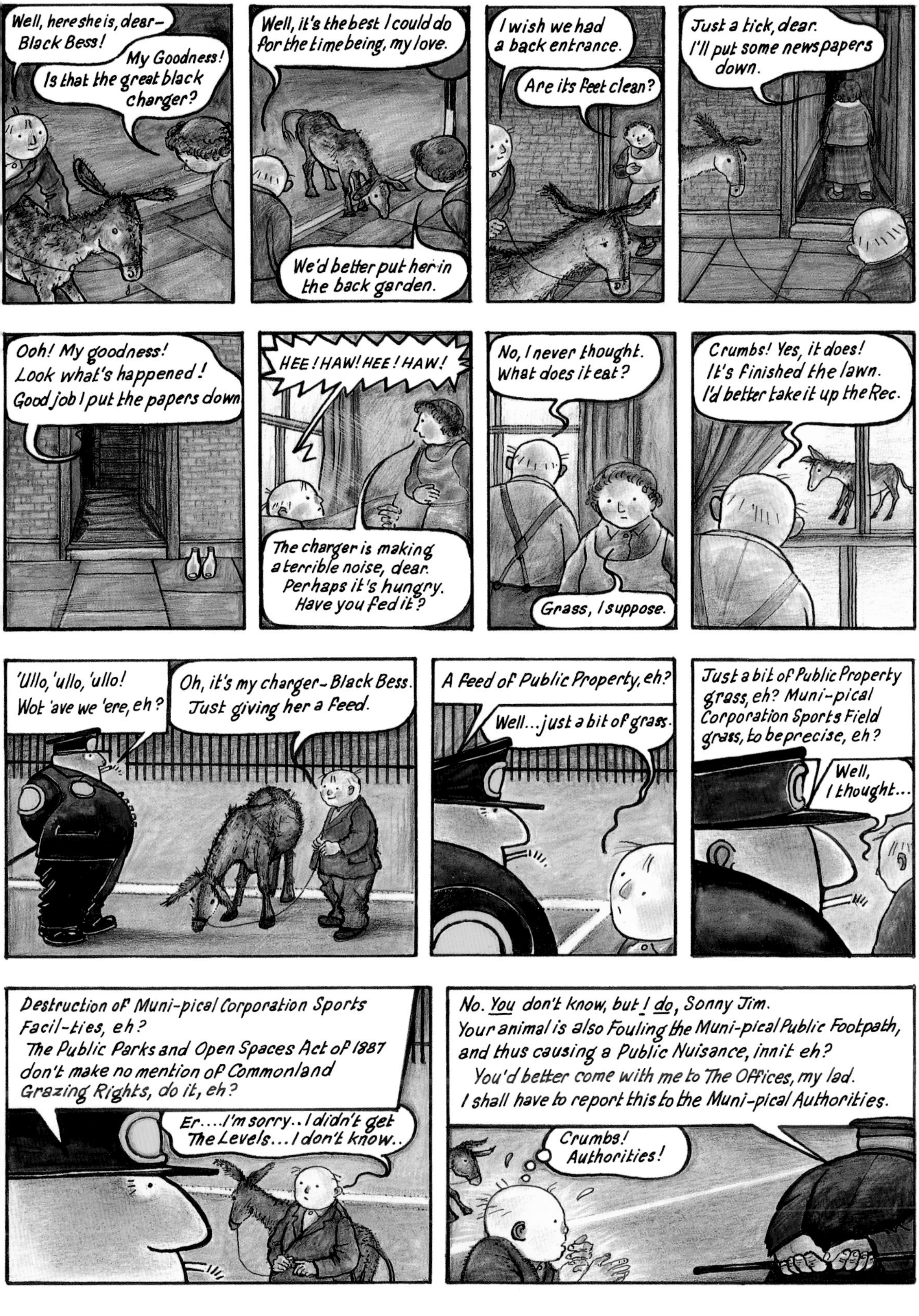
Well, here she is, dear– Black Bess!
My Goodness! Is that the great black charger?
Well, it's the best I could do for the time being, my love.
We'd better put her in the back garden.
I wish we had a back entrance.
Are its feet clean?
Just a tick, dear. I'll put some newspapers down.
Ooh! My goodness! Look what's happened! Good job I put the papers down
HEE! HAW! HEE! HAW!
The charger is making a terrible noise, dear. Perhaps it's hungry. Have you fed it?
No, I never thought. What does it eat?
Grass, I suppose.
Crumbs! Yes, it does! It's finished the lawn. I'd better take it up the Rec.
'Ullo, 'ullo, 'ullo! Wot 'ave we 'ere, eh?
Oh, it's my charger – Black Bess. Just giving her a feed.
A feed of Public Property, eh?
Well... just a bit of grass.
Just a bit of Public Property grass, eh? Muni-pical Corporation Sports Field grass, to be precise, eh?
Well, I thought...
Destruction of Muni-pical Corporation Sports Facil-ties, eh? The Public Parks and Open Spaces Act of 1887 don't make no mention of Commonland Grazing Rights, do it, eh?
Er....I'm sorry.. I didn't get The Levels... I don't know..
No. You don't know, but I do, Sonny Jim. Your animal is also fouling the Muni-pical Public Footpath, and thus causing a Public Nuisance, innit eh? You'd better come with me to The Offices, my lad. I shall have to report this to the Muni-pical Authorities.
Crumbs! Authorities!

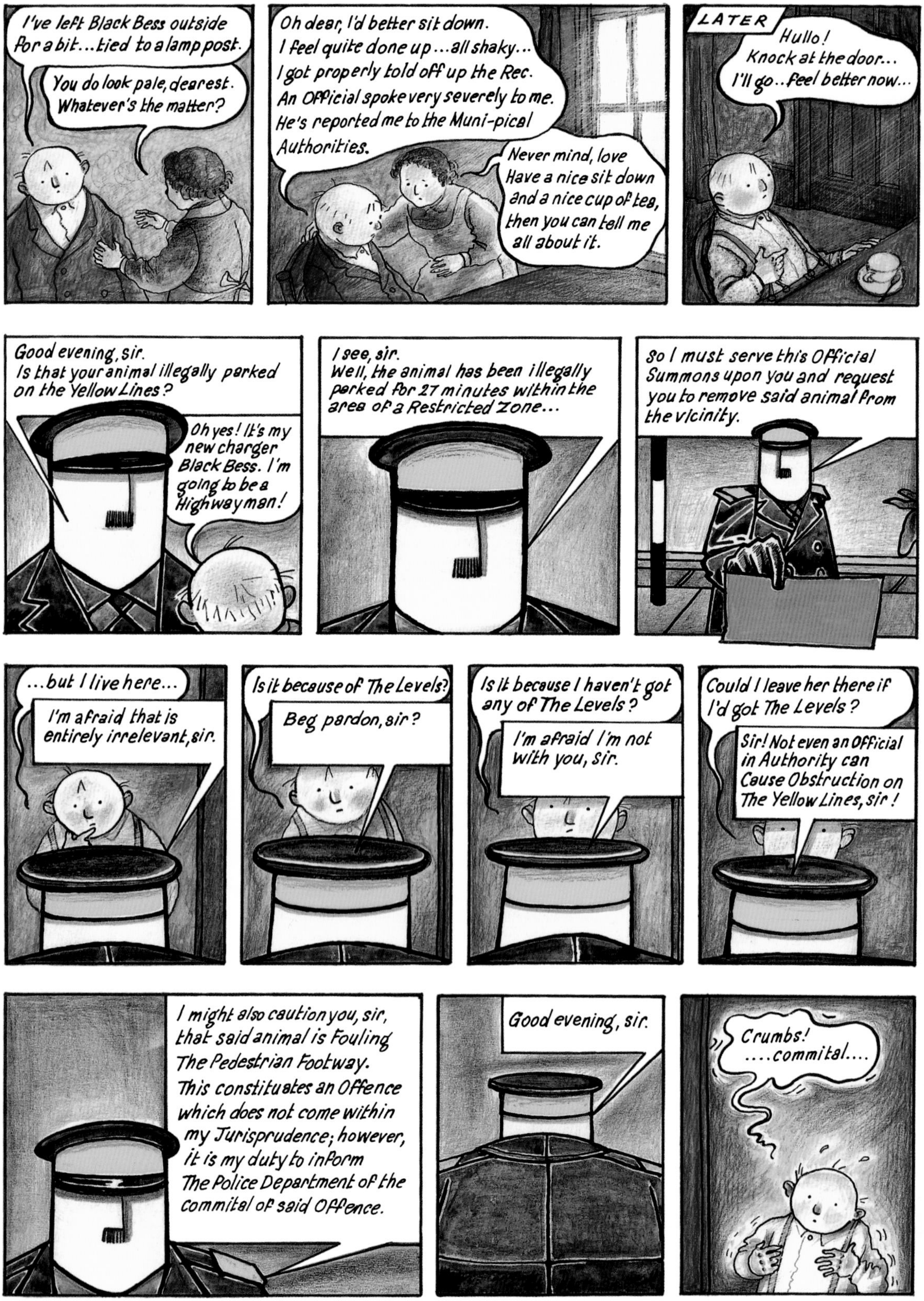
I've left Black Bess outside for a bit... tied to a lamp post.
You do look pale, dearest. Whatever's the matter?
Oh dear, I'd better sit down. I feel quite done up... all shaky... I got properly told off up the Rec. An Official spoke very severely to me. He's reported me to the Muni-pical Authorities.
Never mind, love Have a nice sit down and a nice cup of tea, then you can tell me all about it.
LATER
Hullo! Knock at the door... I'll go.. feel better now...
Good evening, sir. Is that your animal illegally parked on the Yellow Lines?
Oh yes! It's my new charger Black Bess. I'm going to be a Highwayman!
I see, sir. Well, the animal has been illegally parked for 27 minutes within the area of a Restricted Zone...
So I must serve this Official Summons upon you and request you to remove said animal from the vicinity.
...but I live here...
I'm afraid that is entirely irrelevant, sir.
Is it because of The Levels?
Beg pardon, sir?
Is it because I haven't got any of The Levels?
I'm afraid I'm not with you, sir.
Could I leave her there if I'd got The Levels?
Sir! Not even an Official in Authority can Cause Obstruction on The Yellow Lines, sir!
I might also caution you, sir, that said animal is Fouling The Pedestrian Footway. This constitutes an Offence which does not come within my Jurisprudence; however, it is my duty to inform The Police Department of the commital of said Offence.
Good evening, sir.
Crumbs! ....commital....

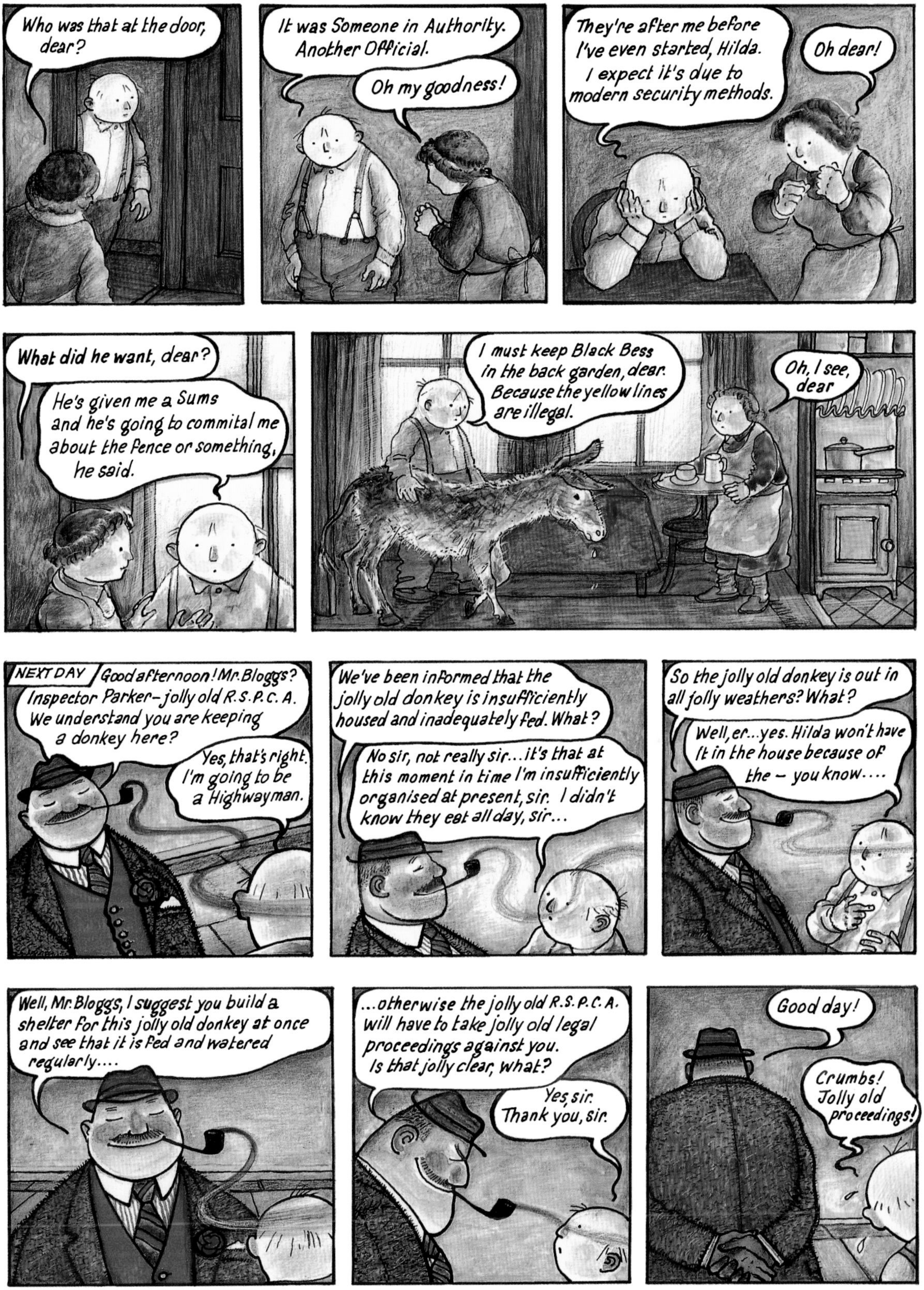
Who was that at the door, dear?
It was Someone in Authority. Another Official.
Oh my goodness!
They're after me before I've even started, Hilda. I expect it's due to modern security methods.
Oh dear!
What did he want, dear?
He's given me a Sums and he's going to commital me about the fence or something, he said.
I must keep Black Bess in the back garden, dear. Because the yellow lines are illegal.
Oh, I see, dear
NEXT DAY
Good afternoon! Mr. Bloggs? Inspector Parker–jolly old R.S.P.C.A. We understand you are keeping a donkey here?
Yes, that's right. I'm going to be a Highwayman.
We've been informed that the jolly old donkey is insufficiently housed and inadequately fed. What?
No sir, not really sir... it's that at this moment in time I'm insufficiently organised at present, sir. I didn't know they eat all day, sir...
So the jolly old donkey is out in all jolly weathers? What?
Well, er... yes. Hilda won't have it in the house because of the – you know....
Well, Mr. Bloggs, I suggest you build a shelter for this jolly old donkey at once and see that it is fed and watered regularly....
...otherwise the jolly old R.S.P.C.A. will have to take jolly old legal proceedings against you. Is that jolly clear, what?
Yes, sir. Thank you, sir.
Good day!
Crumbs! Jolly old proceedings!

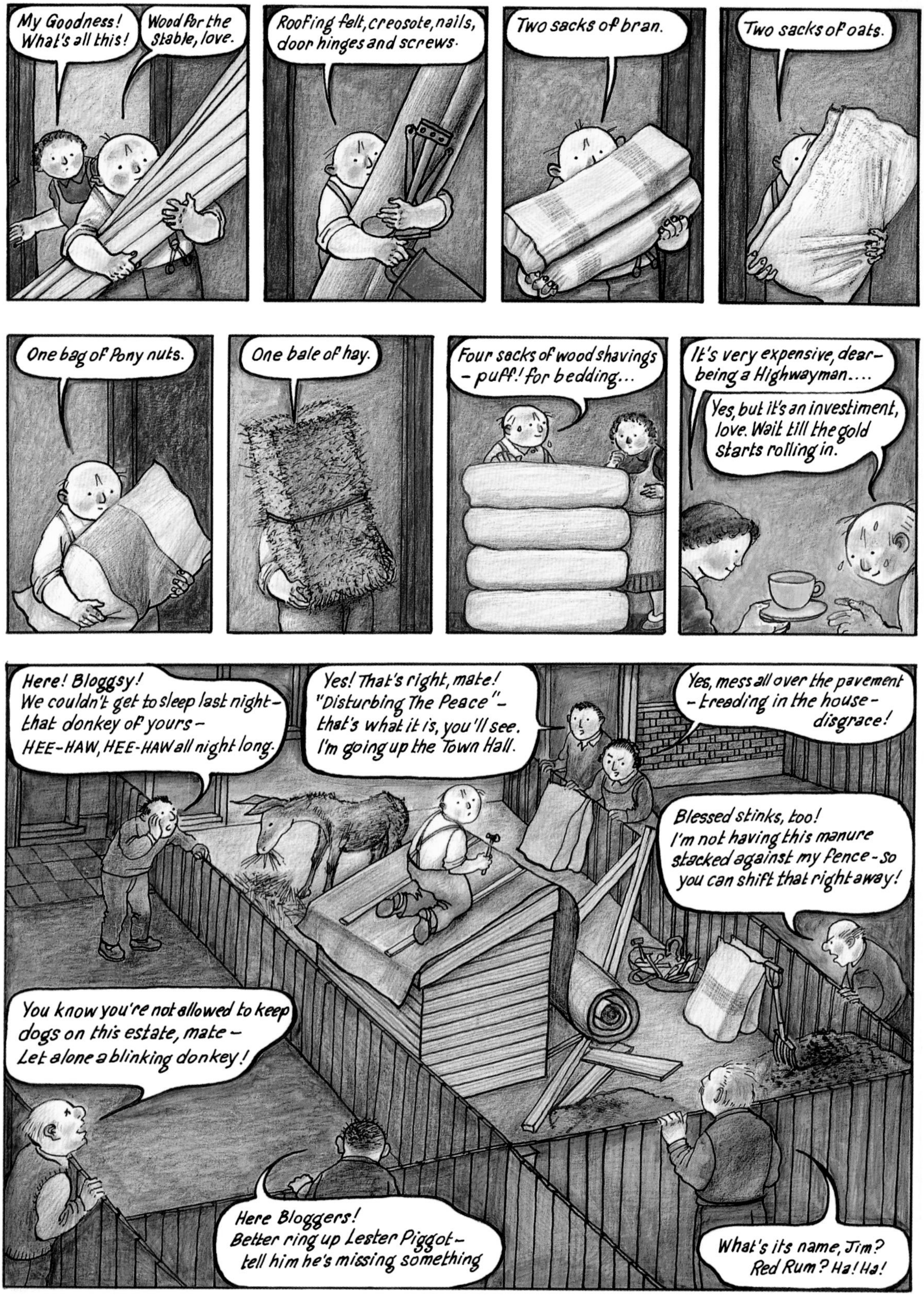
My Goodness! What's all this!
Wood for the stable, love.
Roofing felt, creosote, nails, door hinges and screws.
Two sacks of bran.
Two sacks of oats.
One bag of Pony nuts.
One bale of hay.
Four sacks of wood shavings - puff! for bedding...
It's very expensive, dear - being a Highwayman....
Yes, but it's an investiment, love. Wait till the gold starts rolling in.
Here! Bloggsy! We couldn't get to sleep last night - that donkey of yours - HEE-HAW, HEE-HAW all night long.
Yes! That's right, mate! "Disturbing The Peace" - that's what it is, you'll see. I'm going up the Town Hall.
Yes, mess all over the pavement - treading in the house - disgrace!
Blessed stinks, too! I'm not having this manure stacked against my fence - so you can shift that right away!
You know you're not allowed to keep dogs on this estate, mate - Let alone a blinking donkey!
Here Bloggers! Better ring up Lester Piggot - tell him he's missing something
What's its name, Jim? Red Rum? Ha! Ha!

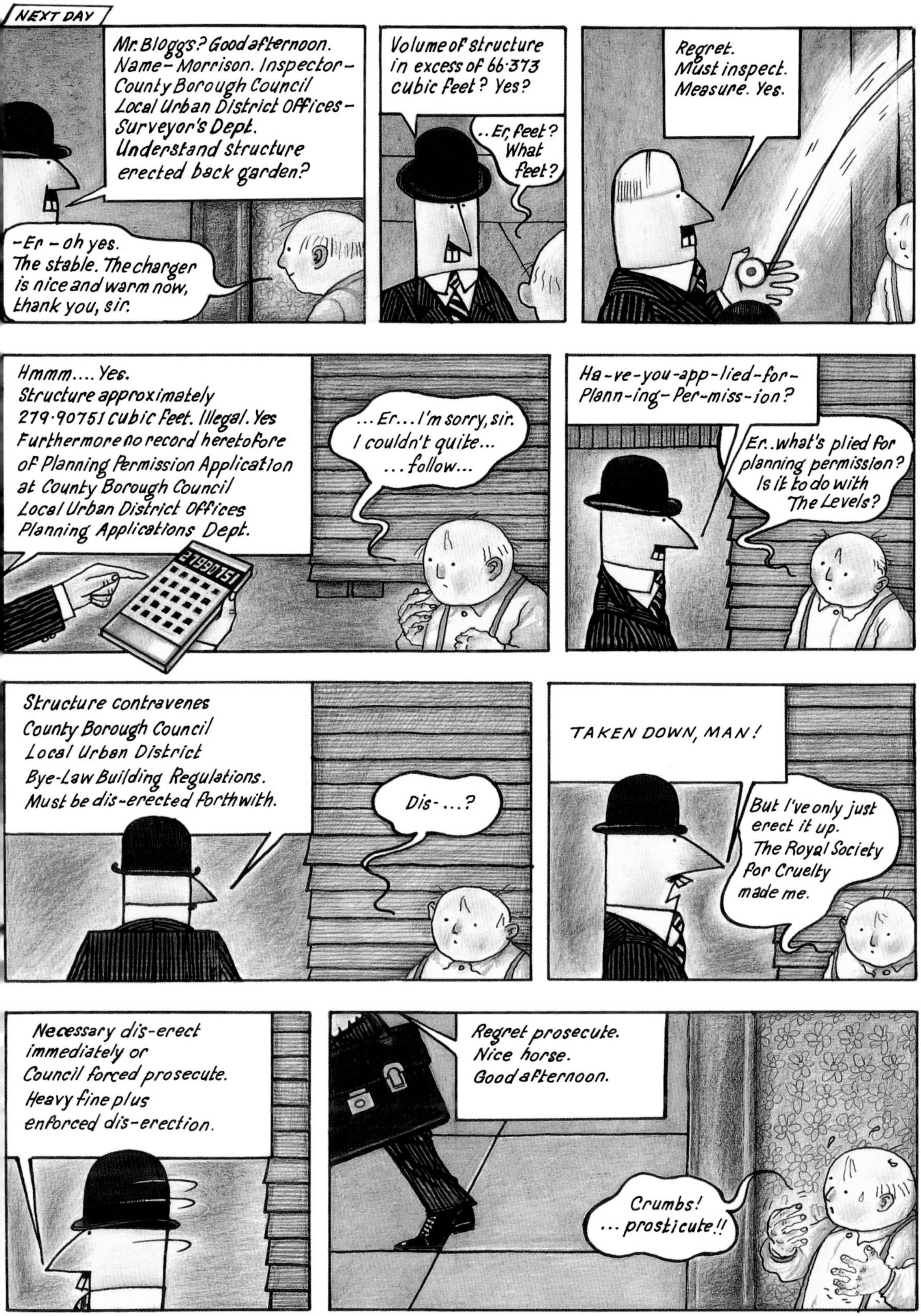
NEXT DAY
Mr. Bloggs? Good afternoon. Name – Morrison. Inspector – County Borough Council Local Urban District Offices – Surveyor's Dept. Understand structure erected back garden?
–Er – oh yes. The stable. The charger is nice and warm now, thank you, sir.
Volume of structure in excess of 66·373 cubic feet? Yes?
..Er, feet? What feet?
Regret. Must inspect. Measure. Yes.
Hmmm.... Yes. Structure approximately 279·90751 cubic feet. Illegal. Yes Furthermore no record heretofore of Planning Permission Application at County Borough Council Local Urban District Offices Planning Applications Dept.
...Er...I'm sorry, sir. I couldn't quite... ...follow...
Ha-ve-you-app-lied-for-Plann-ing-Per-miss-ion?
Er..what's plied for planning permission? Is it to do with The Levels?
Structure contravenes County Borough Council Local Urban District Bye-Law Building Regulations. Must be dis-erected forthwith.
Dis-...?
TAKEN DOWN, MAN!
But I've only just erect it up. The Royal Society for Cruelty made me.
Necessary dis-erect immediately or Council forced prosecute. Heavy fine plus enforced dis-erection.
Regret prosecute. Nice horse. Good afternoon.
Crumbs! ...prosticute!!

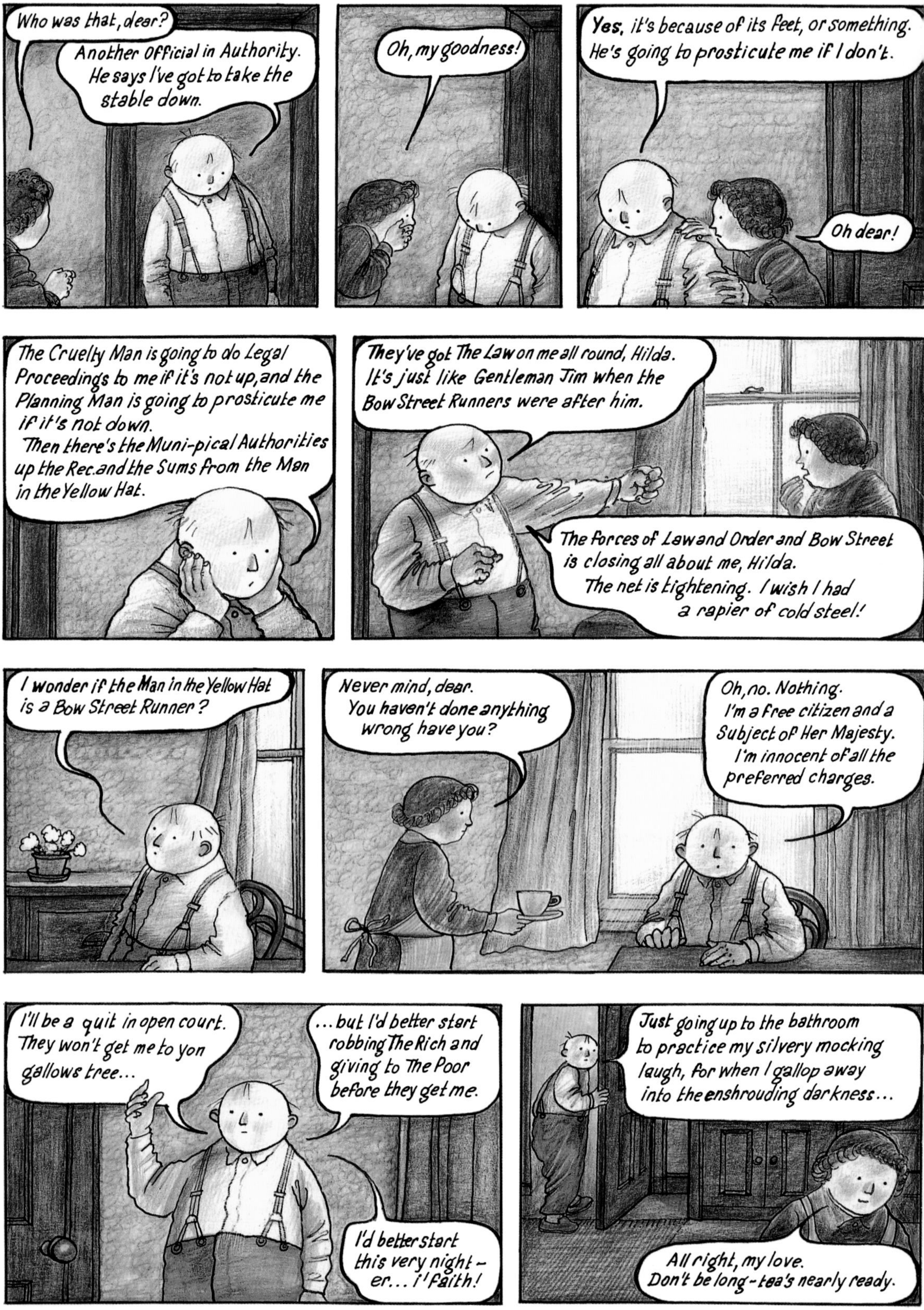
Who was that, dear?
Another Official in Authority. He says I've got to take the stable down.
Oh, my goodness!
Yes, it's because of its feet, or something. He's going to prosticute me if I don't.
Oh dear!
The Cruelty Man is going to do Legal Proceedings to me if it's not up, and the Planning Man is going to prosticute me if it's not down. Then there's the Muni-pical Authorities up the Rec. and the Sums from the Man in the Yellow Hat.
They've got The Law on me all round, Hilda. It's just like Gentleman Jim when the Bow Street Runners were after him.
The forces of Law and Order and Bow Street is closing all about me, Hilda. The net is tightening. I wish I had a rapier of cold steel!
I wonder if the Man in the Yellow Hat is a Bow Street Runner?
Never mind, dear. You haven't done anything wrong have you?
Oh, no. Nothing. I'm a free citizen and a Subject of Her Majesty. I'm innocent of all the preferred charges.
I'll be a quit in open court. They won't get me to yon gallows tree...
...but I'd better start robbing The Rich and giving to The Poor before they get me.
I'd better start this very night – er... i'faith!
Just going up to the bathroom to practice my silvery mocking laugh, for when I gallop away into the enshrouding darkness...
All right, my love. Don't be long – tea's nearly ready.

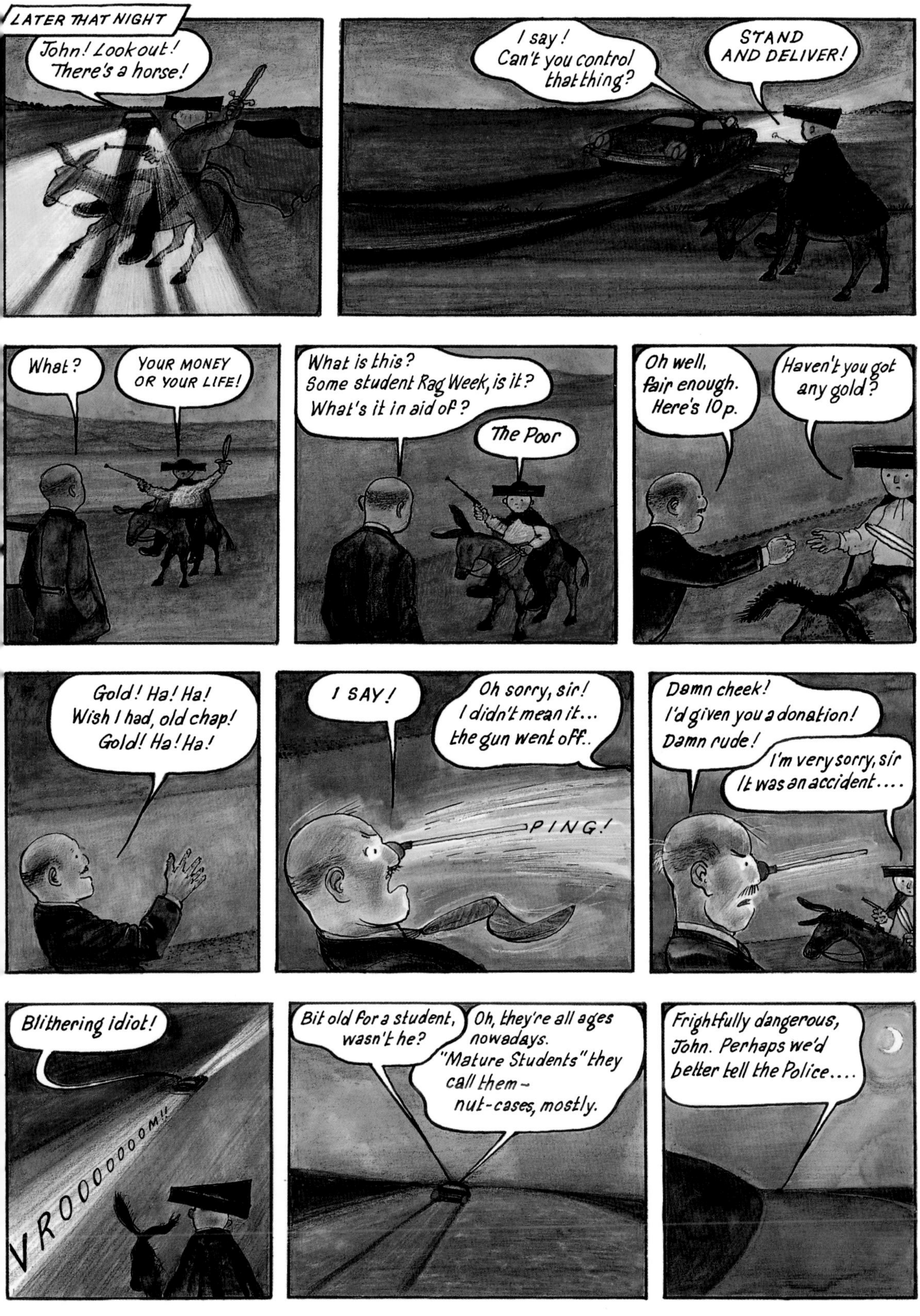

LATER THAT NIGHT
John! Look out! There's a horse!
I say! Can't you control that thing?
STAND AND DELIVER!
What?
YOUR MONEY OR YOUR LIFE!
What is this? Some student Rag Week, is it? What's it in aid of?
The Poor
Oh well, fair enough. Here's 10p.
Haven't you got any gold?
Gold! Ha! Ha! Wish I had, old chap! Gold! Ha! Ha!
I SAY!
Oh sorry, sir! I didn't mean it... the gun went off..
PING!
Damn cheek! I'd given you a donation! Damn rude!
I'm very sorry, sir It was an accident....
Blithering idiot!
VROOOOOOOOM!!
Bit old for a student, wasn't he?
Oh, they're all ages nowadays. "Mature Students" they call them – nut-cases, mostly.
Frightfully dangerous, John. Perhaps we'd better tell the Police....

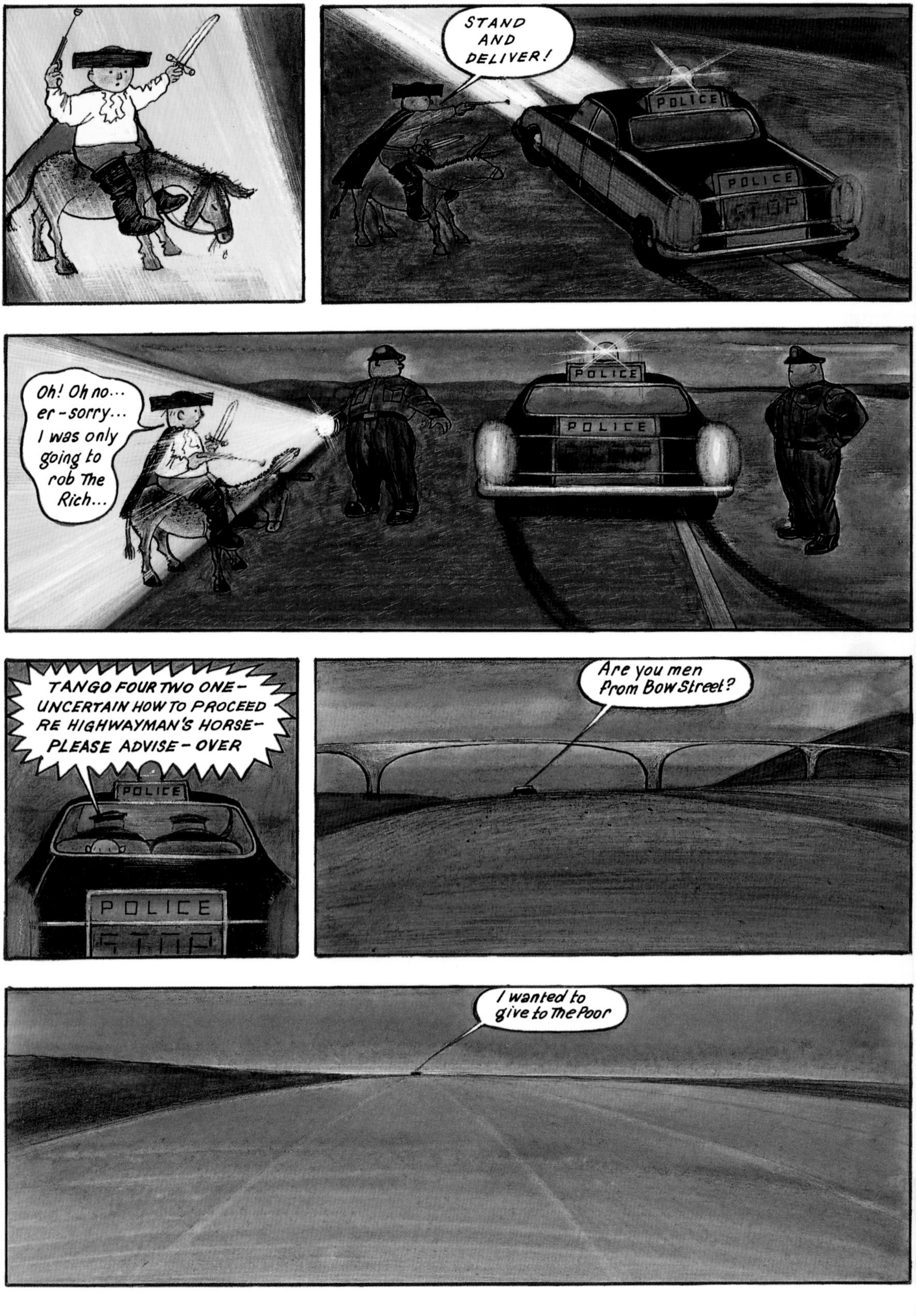
STAND AND DELIVER!
POLICE
POLICE
STOP
Oh! Oh no... er-sorry... I was only going to rob The Rich...
POLICE
POLICE
TANGO FOUR TWO ONE - UNCERTAIN HOW TO PROCEED RE HIGHWAYMAN'S HORSE - PLEASE ADVISE - OVER
POLICE
POLICE
Are you men from Bow Street?
I wanted to give to The Poor

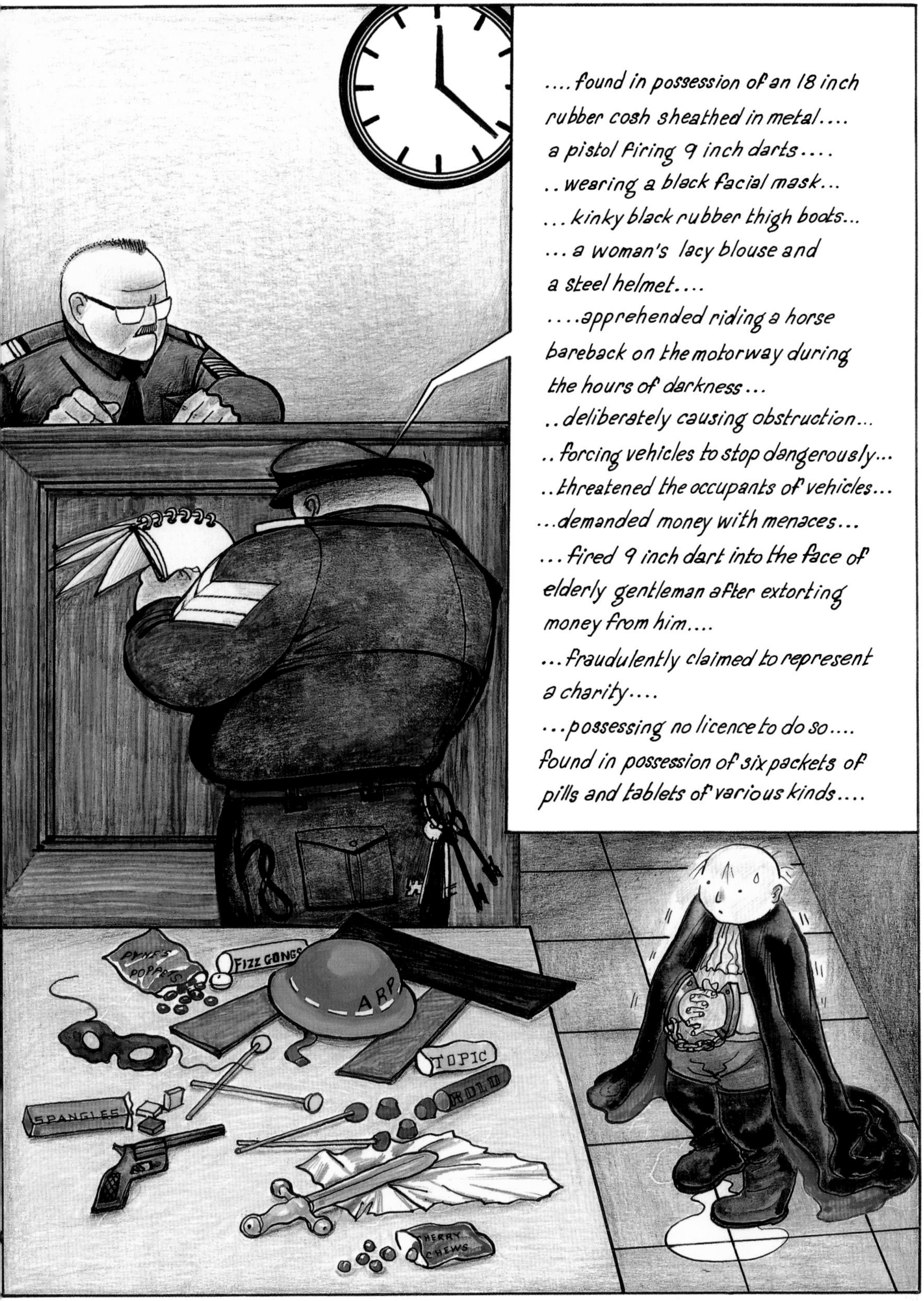

....found in possession of an 18 inch rubber cosh sheathed in metal.... a pistol firing 9 inch darts.... ..wearing a black facial mask... ...kinky black rubber thigh boots... ...a woman's lacy blouse and a steel helmet.... ....apprehended riding a horse bareback on the motorway during the hours of darkness... ..deliberately causing obstruction... ..forcing vehicles to stop dangerously... ..threatened the occupants of vehicles... ...demanded money with menaces... ...fired 9 inch dart into the face of elderly gentleman after extorting money from him.... ...fraudulently claimed to represent a charity.... ...possessing no licence to do so.... found in possession of six packets of pills and tablets of various kinds....
FIZZ GONGS
ARP
TOPIC
ROLO
SPANGLES

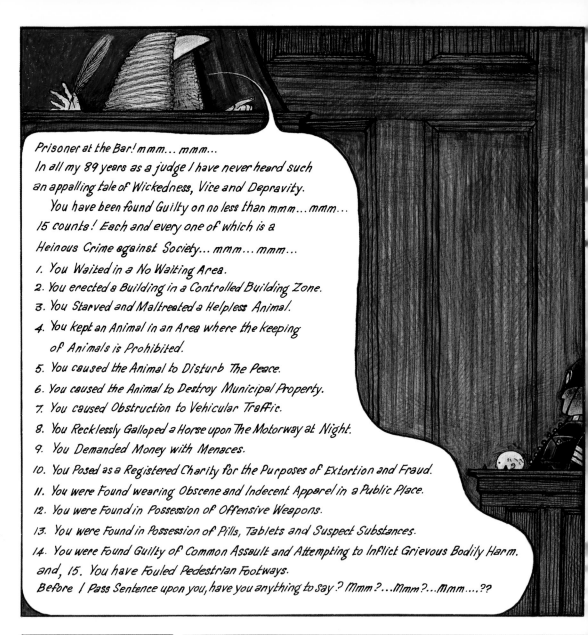

Prisoner at the Bar! mmm... mmm...
In all my 89 years as a judge I have never heard such an appalling tale of Wickedness, Vice and Depravity.
You have been found Guilty on no less than mmm...mmm... 15 counts! Each and every one of which is a Heinous Crime against Society... mmm...mmm...

1. You Waited in a No Waiting Area.
2. You erected a Building in a Controlled Building Zone.
3. You Starved and Maltreated a Helpless Animal.
4. You kept an Animal in an Area where the keeping of Animals is Prohibited.
5. You caused the Animal to Disturb The Peace.
6. You caused the Animal to Destroy Municipal Property.
7. You caused Obstruction to Vehicular Traffic.
8. You Recklessly Galloped a Horse upon The Motorway at Night.
9. You Demanded Money with Menaces.
10. You Posed as a Registered Charity for the Purposes of Extortion and Fraud.
11. You were Found wearing Obscene and Indecent Apparel in a Public Place.
12. You were Found in Possession of Offensive Weapons.
13. You were Found in Possession of Pills, Tablets and Suspect Substances.
14. You were Found Guilty of Common Assault and Attempting to Inflict Grievous Bodily Harm.
and, 15. You have Fouled Pedestrian Footways.
Before I Pass Sentence upon you, have you anything to say? Mmm?...Mmm?...Mmm....??

...er...p..p..please, s...sir I..m..might have b..been. a..b.. better citizen if I'd had The L..L..Levels, sir...

What did you say?

WILL THE PRISONER PLEASE SPEAK UP!

..if I'd h..had L.. L..Levels, your Honours..

What is he saying for Heaven's Sake?

I'm afraid I've no idea, m'lud.

Dammit! It's nearly lunch time!

Then all that remains is for me...mmm to Pass Sentence upon you...mmm mm..bearing in mind your 37 years exemplary employment in-ah...er ...in...in your place of employment, I will be lenient with you...mmm...

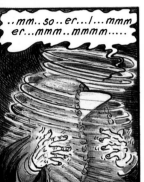

..mm..so..er..I...mmm er...mmm..mmmm.....

I... I... the........Sentence of the Court.... upon you is That you Be Taken from This Place to an Awful Prison-er-Lawful Prison and thence to a PLACE of EXECUTION and That you There be HANGED BY THE NECK UNTIL YE BE DEAD!!!

M'LUD!!! M'LUD!!!

..oh..er..no... I...I...I'll... start again...

Heh! Heh! Those were the days!

Now...mmm..where was I???.... Ah yes...mmm?...the sentence?... I sentence you to be detained During Her Majesty's Pleasure pending a Psychologist's Report..

Beg p'don, m'lud

Yes, what is it?

Not psychologist m'lud-psychiatrist

I said psychiatrist, dammit!

Yes, m'lud Of course m'lud Beg p'don m'lud

As I was saying...Her Majesty's Pleasure etcetera ....pending a psycho-thingummy's report ....take him away....

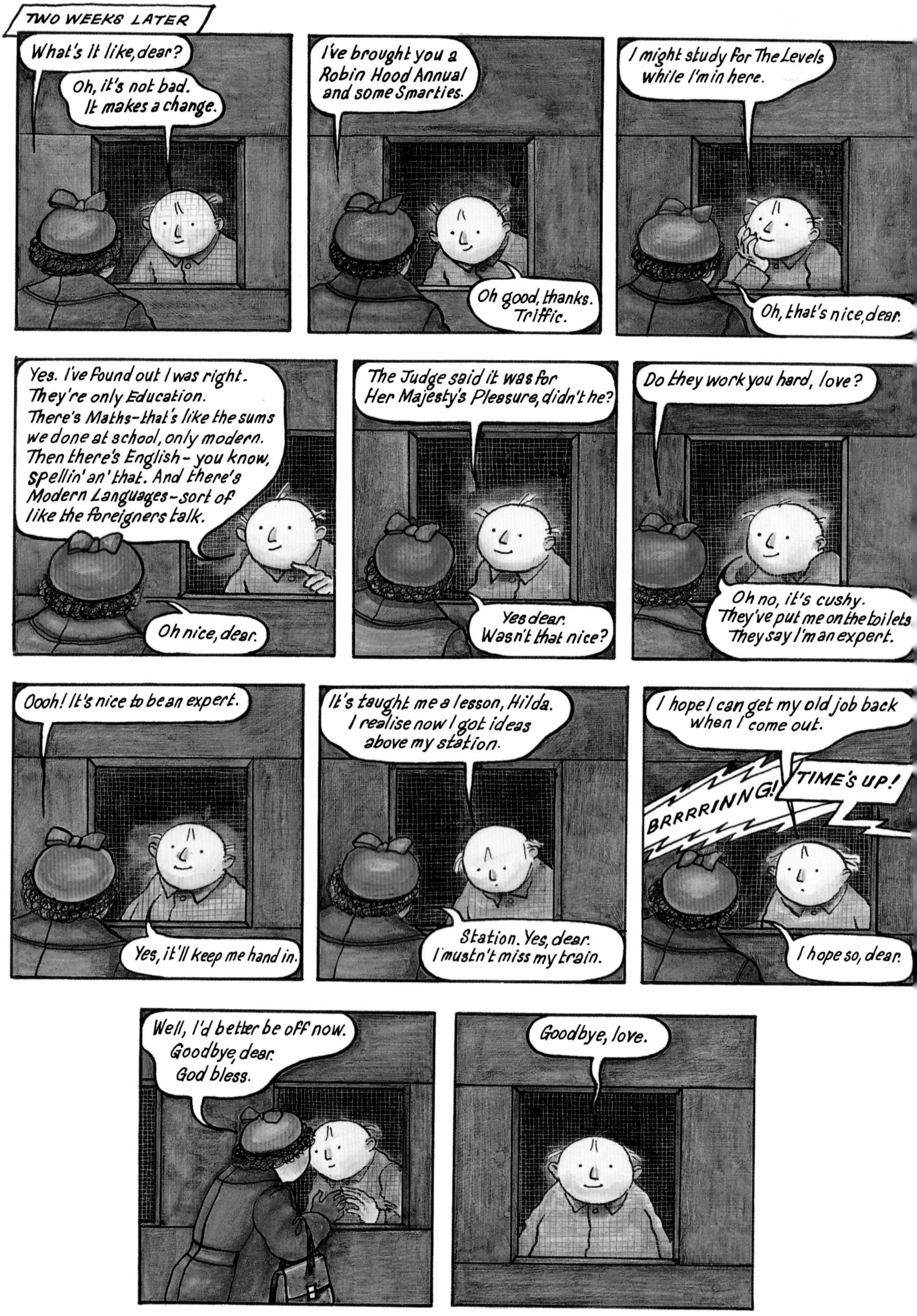
TWO WEEKS LATER
What's it like, dear?
Oh, it's not bad. It makes a change.
I've brought you a Robin Hood Annual and some Smarties.
Oh good, thanks. Triffic.
I might study for The Levels while I'm in here.
Oh, that's nice, dear.
Yes. I've found out I was right. They're only Education. There's Maths - that's like the sums we done at school, only modern. Then there's English - you know, spellin' an' that. And there's Modern Languages - sort of like the foreigners talk.
Oh nice, dear.
The Judge said it was for Her Majesty's Pleasure, didn't he?
Yes dear. Wasn't that nice?
Do they work you hard, love?
Oh no, it's cushy. They've put me on the toilets. They say I'm an expert.
Oooh! It's nice to be an expert.
Yes, it'll keep me hand in.
It's taught me a lesson, Hilda. I realise now I got ideas above my station.
Station. Yes, dear. I mustn't miss my train.
I hope I can get my old job back when I come out.
BRRRRINNG!
TIME'S UP!
I hope so, dear.
Well, I'd better be off now. Goodbye, dear. God bless.
Goodbye, love.